The
Feng Shui
Matrix

The
Feng Shui
Matrix

Another Way to Inherit the Earth

Kartar Diamond

Four Pillars Publishing
CULVER CITY, CALIFORNIA

Although the author and publisher have made every effort to ensure the accuracy and completeness of information contained in this book, we assume no responsibility for errors, inaccuracies, omissions, or any inconsistency herein. Any slights of people, places, or organizations are unintentional.

First printing 2006

ISBN-13: 978-0-9671937-9-3
ISBN-10: 0-9671937-9-6
LCCN: 2005928311

ATTENTION CORPORATIONS, UNIVERSITIES, COLLEGES, AND PROFES-SIONAL ORGANIZATIONS: Quantity discounts are available on bulk purchases of this book for educational, gift purposes, or as premiums for increasing magazine subscriptions or renewals. Special books or book excerpts can also be created to fit specific needs. For information, please contact Four Pillars Publishing, 3824 Perham Drive, Culver City, CA 90232; 310-842-8870.

TABLE OF CONTENTS

ACKNOWLEDGMENTS

I would like to thank Master Larry Sang, for your persistent support and wisdom regarding feng shui, as well as human nature and matters of the heart.

I must also thank my clients, for allowing me into your homes and businesses, your faith in the reality of feng shui principles, and our continuing journey together.

Thank you also to Athena and Lynda Abdo for your clear illustrations and to Lorraine Wilcox for your expertise in content editing.

INTRODUCTION

When I was a young teen in the early 1970s, I was enthralled with a rock star named Leon Russell. I had the obligatory poster of him over my bed and even joined his fan club. Leon Russell had a nickname, at least when he was performing with Joe Cocker (Mad Dogs and Englishmen Tour); Leon was called the "Master of Time and Space."

I find it ironic, that thirty years later, I am attempting in my own way to be a Master of Time and Space. Classical feng shui is referred to as Time and Space School. One of the goals of this book is to show you how to take advantage of opportune moments in time and space.

If a man wants to be successful, he needs to be one step ahead of time and space. And if a woman wants to be successful, she must be one step ahead of a man.

Studies have shown that people who write down their goals are more likely to achieve them, and people who recite their goals out loud are even more likely to manifest them. I have sometimes *exceeded* my goals, and I truly believe I owe some of that success to having learned how to manage aspects of time and space within the realm of feng shui.

Some of my own definitions of feng shui will be sprinkled throughout this book. I hope to intrigue those of you who are new to the subject as well as to invigorate those of you who are already familiar with both the concepts and formulas.

Merriam-Webster Dictionary defines
Ma-trix (Geological)
Pronunciation: mA-triks
Function: noun

1. Something within or from which something else originates, develops or takes form
2. The natural material (as soil or rock) in which something (as a fossil or crystal) is embedded
3. The intercellular substance in which tissue cells (as of connective tissue) are embedded

Cambridge University Press defines:
Matrix (Mathematics)

1. A group of numbers or other symbols arranged in a rectangle which can be used together as a single unit to solve particular mathematical problems

Feng Shui Matrix
Kartar's definition:

1. Something extraordinary, hidden, or embedded in plain view in the ordinary or mundane
2. An array of mathematical computations, which in part or in whole, reveal an energy field that connects more than one plane of existence and influences the human condition
3. A mathematical model for time-space reality and its cyclical effects
4. The relationship between nature and manmade creations (such as climate and architecture) with predictable results on the individual inhabitant as well as groups of people

It would have been a smart marketing tool for me to have titled this second book, *More Feng Shui for Skeptics*; in the world of advertising this is called "branding." But frankly, I'm not that skeptical nor did I want to be known as the feng shui expert on a stubborn crusade to challenge the skeptics of the world about whether feng shui is real or not.

In a world that is becoming more and more polarized in political and religious views, a world where technology has taken its toll on nature, a world where the extremes of yin and yang and unbalanced environments are on the front page of every daily newspaper, my hope is to share with you little jewels of wisdom from a very ancient practice (which is even *more* relevant today because we have more people on the planet). I want to help you be happier, healthier, and more prosperous. As a person who always seems to be living an alternative lifestyle within an alternative lifestyle, I want to delight you with more classical feng shui and to pick up where *Feng Shui for Skeptics* left off.

CHAPTER ONE

Surreal Estate 101

There's a book by Bob Frissell titled *Nothing in This Book Is True, But It's Exactly How Things Are*. He weaves together popular New Age beliefs, sacred geometry, government conspiracy theories, proof of aliens, and crop circles with techniques for altered states of consciousness, energy healing, and time/dimension travel. When I was wracking my brain for a good feng shui book title, I was tempted to borrow his! One underlying message in his book is that even things that seem totally outlandish or impossible could, in fact, be absolutely true.

Feng shui is actually not outlandish at all; rather, it is a concept to which most people can relate on some level because we are all influenced by our environment, if not in the long-term then at least in the short-term. Feng shui is an ancient body of knowledge that can be used to balance a person's surroundings. The result is that he or she can better achieve their goals and have a more fulfilled life. This is no more mysterious than a person balancing his or her diet so he or she has more physical energy, less disease, and better mental concentration.

Many people have now learned some sound principles for what constitutes "good feng shui" in any given environment. But what remains confusing to most new students of feng shui, and certainly for casual readers of the subject, is how to prioritize the information and how to manifest these ideals in real life. For example, if you have learned that the fire element is good to have in a certain area of your house, how do you go about creating an adequate representation of the fire element? And will it be good to have the fire element there all of the time?

Many feng shui enthusiasts as well as serious students are grappling with this huge body of knowledge that also reveals contradictions. Flying Star practitioners sometimes disagree on which "set of numbers" is more powerful. These numbers, which represent energy patterns, are assigned to a house based on when it was built. But there can be another layer of influence based on the current era that we live in. Continuously changing yearly and monthly influences also cycle through each structure. In my opinion, all of these influences should be factored in. Thus, the feng shui matrix becomes a parallel universe that is ever present and ever changing.

My goals in writing *The Feng Shui Matrix* are to enhance your understanding of authentic feng shui, to help you prioritize the information you have been exposed to, and to dispense some powerful remedies that are usually handed down directly from master to student, and not as commonly known or written about. Some of you reading this book may have already been exposed to the various formulas, but I guarantee my interpretation of the formula will be worthy of considering.

After receiving so much positive feedback from *Feng Shui for Skeptics*, it was immediately obvious readers were hungry for even more easy-to-use formulas and real case study examples. And as I stated in the last pages of my first book, the questions that come up seem endless. The more you learn, the more humble you can become.

Once again, I have not attempted to explain classical feng shui from A to Z in a rigid kind of order, and certainly not the order in which it is usually taught to the serious student. But instead I've put forth to you formulas and remedies that stand on their own, which are *not* necessarily hinged on you having any previous formal training.

Throughout the book, I will go back and forth with remedies that come from several different schools of feng shui. We will dabble in easy formulas that come directly from Chinese astrology as they relate to a house and your personal relationship with your house, as well as tidbits from the Eight Mansion School of feng shui. These are personal remedies that will work for you and not for someone else born in a different year. They both use distinct methods for determining ways to use your birth data.

I will also share with you insight from the Flying Star School for areas of life that are related to timing. For instance, you can predict which year you are more likely to attract romance in your life and then further stimulate that with a remedy. "Form School" theories will be further explained for their own merit, as well as how they work in conjunction with the other schools.

Important Note: Throughout this book there are references to different house types. It should be understood that most of the time, the interpretation of a house (an actual personal residence) will be similar when used to evaluate a commercial property. If I use the word "house" in describing where the occupants could have a certain problem, that same situation can exist in a work environment if the structure has the same shape, orientation, or physical features. So instead of describing the same structure type each time respectively as a house and/or a building, I will just refer to any structure as a "house."

The subtitle of this book, *Another Way to Inherit the Earth* was conceived just by thinking about the various reasons why people seek out the services of a feng shui master or why people are intrigued enough just to read about it.

Empowering your life means different things to different people. But with few exceptions, most people desire the three universal basics: *more money, more love,* and *better health,* usually in that order. Money (as a means to another end), love, and health are all manifestations of energy and consciousness. Some people believe that energy (like money) is finite and should be shared more equitably, while others believe that energy is infinite and everyone can tap into as much of it as they want.

The Biblical phrase, "the meek shall inherit the Earth," implies (in my understanding) that the truly good-hearted, nonaggressive, worthy souls will eventually get all the goodies, rewards, and blessings at some later point in time and place, as long as they adhere to compassionate and selfless values while on Earth.

A literal inheritance is a gift of money, real estate or possessions given by a relative or friend, passed along to the next generation. *From a feng shui perspective, we all inherit the entire Earth, over and over again.* Earth contains everything we need to be happy and fulfilled. Just think about how so many medical answers and cures to our ailments exists right here in the plant and mineral kingdom on this Earth. Earth itself is filled with information, power, and love.

The whole body of wisdom I call feng shui is like an owner's manual for how to best deal with the energies of this Earth, the stars that influence us, our climates, and seasons. When we say, "Let nature take its course," we are acknowledging the innate intelligence and cyclical predictability of life on this planet. Feng shui is just an aspect or dimension of nature.

The general public still may not know; however, that feng shui theory and applications could address a specific issue or incident like being in an accident or a mother- and daughter-in-law not getting along with each other. What has always intrigued me about feng shui is how very personal and specific it can be when applied correctly. In the same way that a human being might suffer from something serious such as schizophrenia (in part due to a vitamin deficiency), an unbalanced environment can also cause a specific disturbance or event in the lives of people who dwell in that unbalanced space.

What you want in your life could be very different than what someone else wants. But whatever you consider "success" in your life, your environment can help you or it can hinder you. We understand this instinctually when we refer to someone as an "underachiever" or an "overachiever." The implication is that somebody is doing better or worse than expected in their life, based on their upbringing, family, economic, or geographic circumstances. We are thus acknowledging that environment affects us all.

Feng shui cannot necessarily change a destiny, but it can help you create a supportive environment, so that no matter what else you need to experience, at least your personal environment will be working for you, instead of against you.

We have that old saying, "your home should be your castle," and the ideal home would serve as a retreat from the harshness and chaos of the outside world.

How Much Does Feng Shui Affect Us?

Even the most enthusiastic practitioner knows there are a multitude of influences on your life, and you can't blame bad feng shui for everything that goes wrong, or credit good feng shui for everything that goes your way.

If it is not your destiny to be Mick Jagger or Magic Johnson, then feng shui remedies will not catapult you into that stratosphere of stardom. People are usually born leaders, trendsetters, or with a destiny for celebrity. But how many of us truly live to our greatest potential? As human beings, we still use only a small percentage of our brains. There are so many possibilities ahead of us in terms of how we can harness the energies of our environment and how much more perceptive and sophisticated we can become. The science fiction of today may easily become the science facts of tomorrow.

Things happen to people all the time where they feel like there has been some kind of divine intervention. But has their destiny really changed? Even with dramatic improvements in your life as the result of feng shui remedies, you are still living within your ultimate destiny. Some people do not even have it in their destiny to meet the right people at the right time, to change their luck. Free will may be limited to a handful of experiences or opportunities that will still ultimately lead you to the same destiny. This may be like traveling along different but parallel paths. When a feng shui master forewarns you about some dangers that may lie ahead, you are already in a better luck phase just to have been forewarned and given the tools to take yourself into another direction.

Your total environment has a tremendous impact on you in both obvious and nonobvious ways. Sure, there are people who can excel in spite of all types of adversity, including bad feng shui, but in my own records of client cases, I rarely see anyone doing poorly who has a good feng shui environment. As well, I rarely see someone doing fantastic in a bad feng shui environment.

One of my friends, who is also a feng shui consultant, was looking for a new place to live. She was being rather fanatical about her high standards of what she was looking for in a new home. We discussed how even my own home was not perfect and how I might even rank it as only B+. I wanted her to not worry about finding perfection, since it is rarely out there, already built to our high standards. She then explained to me that she knew through her personal Chinese astrology analysis that her personal luck was going to be very bad for another ten years. For her, having a perfect feng shui environment seemed essential to help compensate for what she calculated to be some rough years ahead of her. When you know both feng shui and personal astrology, then you can have a powerful and realistic perspective of your life and potential.

How you handle your circumstances, spiritual outlook, and habits will also appear to influence the direction you are going. For example, I have lived in some houses that definitely presented the possibilities of attracting legal problems. I could have chosen to retaliate and sue over a number of injustices set against me, and these legal problems could have escalated. But as a conscious practice of "letting go" and trying not to focus on the negative, I let things slide without taking legal action. One good question to ask yourself when you are in the heat of the moment or extremely upset about something is, "How am I going to feel about this several years from now?" Or "Am I even going to re-member this person who has just hurt me or insulted me?"

I always appreciate it when someone has been unduly slandered in the press and the comment from the slandered party is that he or she is "not going to dignify it with a response." This is an example of applied intelligence. You don't have to fight fire with fire, in other words. Some people are intelligent but do stupid things. They don't apply their intel-ligence to come up with a creative solution. I have found that giving myself the perspective of fast-forwarding into the future helps to diffuse my heat-of-the-moment frustrations. An old military concept is to "keep your enemies close so you know what they are doing." This may be the art of war or the art of feng shui; give yourself the gift of patience to see how time and space unfold in front of you. It is the essence of "going with the flow."

For many years I practiced yoga as a way to balance my inner world, which would then affect my outer world. Feng shui works in the reverse format, whereby you balance the outer world so that it will then posi-tively affect your inner world.

Some of our physical reality can be linked to conscious and uncon-scious thoughts or projections. My mother frequently used the mantra, "This makes my blood boil!" I don't think it was a coincidence that she had high blood pressure. Another one of her favorite sayings was, "I need that like a hole in the head!" In the feng shui trigram system (which is covered in this book,) my mother was the "Chien trigram." The Chien trigram is associated with the head. And when Mom was being forced to do something she didn't want to do, she'd frequently say, "I should have my head examined." I also don't think it was a coincidence that she ultimately developed a brain tumor.

Understanding the other components that go into your life, such as destiny, environment and attitude reveals that feng shui constitutes about 20 to 25 percent of your life "molding." Because a lot of people do not apply their intelligence with action, they appear to succumb to their bad feng shui even more. Perhaps with these folks, feng shui may affect them closer to 30 percent. At the same time, I have many spiritual clients who try to live healthy and positive lives, but still seem to experience the full brunt of the bad feng shui in their homes, almost as if their prayers and meditation were speeding up their karma! This is just speculation, but I have seen a lot of kind, spiritual, and aware people still have money problems, health problems, and unhappiness in their relationships, as a direct result of bad feng shui.

When you regularly apply good feng shui principles and practices in your life and surroundings, you can smooth over a lot of rough edges and negative circumstances. And if it is your birth right to inherit the Earth, then you are entitled to a copy of the owner's manual.

The following charts and compass illustration will be very important references throughout the entire book. Some of the recommendations will require that you be familiar with the boundaries of just the eight basic directions. Each direction spans a 45-degree range as well as taking up a certain amount of square footage when the directions are viewed as boxy sections within your home.

The term "quadrant" is used frequently throughout this book and it is a word that is often used to describe a square or rectangular section of a house's floor plan. The word "quadrant" really means "four sections," but it is used loosely here instead to indicate an individual four-sided section within any floor plan. A floor plan can be divided up into nine sections, like a tic-tac-toe grid. Each of these nine boxes can be called a quadrant for feng shui purposes.

Whenever there is a reference to one of the eight basic directions, you will have more space to work with than when the remedies must be applied within a smaller 15-degree range. You can use both charts as a continual guide from chapter to chapter and you will refer back to these charts over and over again. Chapter Two goes step by step in how to use a compass so that you really know where these directions are in relation to your own space.

The Eight Basic Directions, Their Abbreviations and Their 45-Degree Range

North (N)	337.5–22.5 degrees
Northeast (NE)	22.5–67.5 degrees
East (E)	67.5–112.5 degrees
Southeast (SE)	112.5–157.5 degrees
South (S)	157.5–202.5 degrees
Southwest (SW)	202.5–247.5 degrees
West (W)	247.5–292.5 degrees
Northwest (NW)	292.5–337.5 degrees

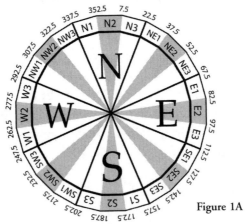

Figure 1A

Figure 1A is a compass illustration that shows not only the eight basic directions as they appear on a compass, but also the three subdivisions within each of the eight basic directions. There are in total twenty-four directions that have 15-degree increments around the compass.

Master Chart Showing the 24 Directions

North: first sector (N1)	337.5–352.5 degrees
North: second sector (N2)	352.5– 7.5 degrees
North: third sector (N3)	7.5– 22.5 degrees
Northeast: first (NE1)	22.5– 37.5 degrees
Northeast: second (NE2)	37.5– 52.5 degrees
Northeast: third (NE3)	52.5– 67.5 degrees
East: first sector (E1)	67.5– 82.5 degrees
East: second secto (E2)	82.5– 97.5 degrees
East: third sector (E3)	97.5– 112.5 degrees
Southeast: first (SE1)	112.5– 127.5 degrees
Southeast: second (SE2)	127.5– 142.5 degrees
Southeast: third (SE3)	142.5– 157.5 degrees
South: first sector (S1)	157.5– 172.5 degrees
South: second sector (S2)	172.5– 187.5 degrees
South: third sector (S3)	187.5– 202.5 degrees
Southwest: first (SW1)	202.5– 217.5 degrees
Southwest: second (SW2)	217.5– 232.5 degrees
Southwest: third (SW3)	232.5– 247.5 degrees
West: first sector (W1)	247.5– 262.5 degrees
West: second sector (W2)	262.5– 277.5 degrees
West: third sector (W3)	277.5– 292.5 degrees
Northwest: first (NW1)	292.5– 307.5 degrees
Northwest: second (NW2)	307.5– 322.5 degrees
Northwest: third (NW3)	322.5– 337.5 degrees

Throughout this book, if there is a reference to a direction, without distinguishing what division of the direction, then it is the *whole* of the direction that you should be concerned with. In other words, southwest (SW) means all of southwest, but SW1 only means the first sector of southwest (202.5– 217.5 degrees.)

Your Best Place to Meditate, Concentrate, or Relax

On the subject of spirituality, everyone has a perfect "meditation direction." This is based on your personal trigram. This personal trigram (also called a gua or kua) is based on what year you were born and your gender. That year and gender are associated with a particular direction. Following is a chart that shows your best direction to meditate.

Refer to the personal trigram chart. There is one for males and another chart for females. You will scroll down to the year you were born and see the name of your trigram and the meditation direction attached to it.

● If you want to know the trigram of someone born before or after the years listed in these charts, you can still compute their personal trigram because they repeat themselves every nine years. Add or

Males: Personal Trigram Chart for Best Meditation Direction

Birth Year	Trigram	Direction	Birth Year	Trigram	Direction
1930, 1939, 1948, 1957	Tui	West	1966, 1975, 1984, 1993	Tui	West
1931, 1940, 1949, 1958	Chien	Northwest	1967, 1976, 1985, 1994	Chien	Northwest
1932, 1941, 1950, 1959	K'un	Southwest	1968, 1977, 1986, 1995	K'un	Southwest
1933, 1942, 1951, 1960	Sun	Southeast	1969, 1978, 1987, 1996	Sun	Southeast
1934, 1943, 1952, 1961	Chen	East	1970, 1979, 1988, 1997	Chen	East
1935, 1944, 1953, 1962	K'un	Southwest	1971, 1980, 1989, 1998	K'un	Southwest
1936, 1945, 1954, 1963	K'an	North	1972, 1981, 1990, 1999	K'an	North
1937, 1946, 1955, 1964	Li	South	1973, 1982, 1991, 2000	Li	South
1938, 1947, 1956, 1965	Ken	Northeast	1974, 1983, 1992, 2001	Ken	Northeast

subtract 9, 18, 27, etc., to any one of these birth years to get their actual birth year and that will be their personal trigram and associated direction as well.

- The beginning of each year, using the feng shui *solar* calendar, begins on February 4, not January 1. So if you were born between January 1 and February 3, subtract one year from your Western year of birth.

- If you can sit with *your back* to that particular direction while meditating or praying, you will be aligning yourself with a more supportive flow of energy.

- If you can utilize the part of your house that is your personal "meditation direction" then that is another way of making the most of your circumstances. This is a literal example of "going with the flow" instead of against it.

Females: Personal Trigram Chart for Best Meditation Direction

Birth Year	Trigram	Direction	Birth Year	Trigram	Direction
1930, 1939, 1948, 1957	Ken	Northeast	1966, 1975, 1984, 1993	Ken	Northeast
1931, 1940, 1949, 1958	Li	South	1967, 1976, 1985, 1994	Li	South
1932, 1941, 1950, 1959	K'an	North	1968, 1977, 1986, 1995	K'an	North
1933, 1942, 1951, 1960	K'un	Southwest	1969, 1978, 1987, 1996	K'un	Southwest
1934, 1943, 1952, 1961	Chen	East	1970, 1979, 1988, 1997	Chen	East
1935, 1944, 1953, 1962	Sun	Southeast	1971, 1980, 1989, 1998	Sun	Southeast
1936, 1945, 1954, 1963	Ken	Northeast	1972, 1981, 1990, 1999	Ken	Northeast
1937, 1946, 1955, 1964	Chien	Northwest	1973, 1982, 1991, 2000	Chien	Northwest
1938, 1947, 1956, 1965	Tui	West	1974, 1983, 1992, 2001	Tui	West

Here is an example: If you were born between February 4, 1961, and February 3, 1962, then you are the Chen trigram whether you are male or female. Chen is the only trigram where gender does not differentiate the personal trigram for that year. The Chen trigram is associated with east. Therefore, sitting with your back to east will enhance the depth of the meditation for the person who is the Chen trigram. (You are the Chen trigram if you were born after February 4 in 1952, 1961, 1970, and 1979.) All the trigrams repeat in nine-year cycles.

There is a difference between *location* and *direction*. A location can be defined within a floor plan, such as the north quadrant of a building. But the direction is how you align your body. For example, you can have two people sitting in an office in the north quadrant of a building. But within the room, they each might position their desks to face each other. So, they would each be facing a different *direction,* while being seated in the same *location* within the building.

After you learn the location of your meditation direction, see if that location is a good spot to sit in and if it is a practical location to use. If you discover that your most peaceful location of the house lands in the bathroom, I do not recommend sitting in the bathtub to meditate! Instead, find an appropriate alternative, which could even be your meditation direction within a room where it is practical. (Individual rooms are miniature versions of the house.)

Not everyone formally meditates. But these directions are still useful for quiet contemplation or for doing something you love that is calming and peaceful, such as sewing or tinkering with some project. This direction that is so good for meditating is also good for peaceful sleep. Sleep with your heading pointing to this direction if you can.

What do you do if you share a bed with someone, but have different best sleeping directions? Often, the limitations of the room layout will dictate that the bed can only go one way realistically. But if there is an opportunity for someone who has not been sleeping well to shift the bed against another usable wall, then go for it. Experiment for your health's sake.

How to See the Invisible Energies Called "Ch'i"

There is an old yogic saying, "If you can't see God *in* all, you can't see God *at* all." Seeing, in this saying, is more metaphorical than actually visually seeing something with your eyes. It is a beautiful statement about trying to achieve unconditional love and not sitting in judgment.

Ch'i in its many manifestations can literally be touched or smelled; it can be sensed, it can be heard; and it can also be seen with a little retraining of the eyes.

As children, we see all kinds of things that adults often dismiss as an immature, active imagination. As we get older, our ability to see other dimensions fades away, much like our memory of past lives or even prebirth experiences. Once I was driving around with my son, who was about six years old at the time. We were talking about food and I was congratulating him on liking to eat many different types of food, when other children his age can be overly fussy in that department.

Even as a six-year-old, he liked food that was a little spicy. He then turned to me and said in a very matter-of-fact way, "The reason I like spicy food, is because you ate so much of it when I was inside of you." This was actually true, although I had never told him about my pregnancy preference for Mexican and Indian food. Could he have had a prebirth memory or experience of what I ate while he was inside me?

Like an awestruck child, where so many things are exciting because they are being experienced for the first time, you need to retrain your eyes. You need to initially approach this retraining in an environment where you can relax and not be distracted. At this point, you may want to follow the suggestions which will be given and then take a break from your reading, or come back to the actual practice of the meditation at another time.

The point of giving out a meditation in this book is to try to give you an experience of altered consciousness that will bring more reality to all the feng shui principles which will follow. As a comparison, imagine trying to read a book about relationships if you had never been in a single one or even to have witnessed someone else in a relationship (like your parents). I do not want your understanding of ch'i to be only intellectual. It should be interactive and experiential. If you are already a very aware person, a meditation practitioner, or have some other kind of metaphysical practice, then none of this will be new to you.

Many people try to alter their reality and perceptions with drugs, herbs, or alcohol. Some substances, used appropriately and in moderation, can work as a portal to higher states of consciousness. But other substances, especially alcohol, will do more damage than good to the body, mind, and spirit. The goal of meditation is to heighten awareness, not dull it. In fact, you can even meditate too much and become a sort of zombie. I used to know people who meditated for many hours a day as a way of avoiding life and responsibilities. This is selfish and dysfunctional behavior, especially if you have a family to take care of.

Instead, one goal of meditation is to recharge your mind so you can in fact be in a state of meditative calm while you carry on with all your mundane activities, especially stressful ones. In the same way that it takes only about fifteen minutes per day of aerobic exercise to enhance your metabolic rate for a good portion of the day, it may take only fifteen to thirty minutes to heighten your awareness for the rest of that day. Thirty minutes might sound like a substantial investment, but compare that to how much television you may be watching and how it affects the quality of your life.

Meditation to See Ch'i

Most of the time, if not all of the time, our physical eyes will focus on objects, near and far. Right now you are looking at the page and the words on this page. When you gaze about a room, your eyes will hone in on the furnishings and decor. What about the *space* between these objects? Start focusing on the space *between* objects.

Let your eyes relax. You might be able to see the movement of the air right in front of you. It may even have flecks of color in it.

Breathe deep as you allow yourself to look at the space in front of you. Once you see the movement of the air, you can even reach out and move your hand through the space. You will then notice the air currents break up their previous pattern of movement and reconfigure themselves, almost the way you can try to upset a trail of ants only to see them reform their line.

If simply pointing out that you should look at *space* instead of objects does not immediately shift the focus of your eyes, you may need to relax more. The following yogic breathing technique will not only help you relax, but it is also generally very good for the glandular system. It can produce a natural high.

Four-Part Breath Meditation
(To Invigorate Your Own Personal Ch'i and to Help You See It)

1. Sit in a relaxed manner on the floor or in a chair, keeping your spine as straight as possible without being tense.

2. Tuck your chin in slightly toward your collar bone, so that your neck is straight, but without being tense.

3. You will begin to ration each breath in four parts or four installments, as if "sipping" the breath, but only through the nose (like sniffing).

4. Inhale in four parts and after only a few rounds of this you will be able to control the amount of oxygen in each "sniff." You want to equally ration the total volume of your lung capacity into four equal parts. You can even keep your mind occupied by counting silently to yourself: 1, 2, 3, and 4 with each sniff of air.

5. Then, exhale the total volume of your lung capacity in four equal parts so that on the fourth part of the exhale your lungs feel completely empty.

6. Continue inhaling in four parts and exhaling in four parts, all the while challenging your lung capacity to increase as you continue with the rounds.

7. Do all breathing through the nose rather than through the mouth. Keep your eyes closed.

8. Continue with this breathing meditation for at least five to eleven minutes, but you can certainly do it longer. The longer you do it, the higher you will get and the easier it will be for you to see the air, see the *ch'i* in front of you once you open your eyes.

9. You can also advance your experience of this meditation by eventually moving up to six parts per breath (inhale six parts and exhale

in six parts) and eventually eight parts inhale and eight parts exhale.

Footnote: When you breathe in this four-part pattern (like pumping air into a bike tire), you will consciously want to move your belly. You will be pumping the breath and directing it to the navel region as you expand a little more with each inhalation. With each *exhalation,* tug in your navel point a little to help push the breath up and out. In order to do this effectively, you do not want any clothing restrictions around your waist. Loosen your pants or do whatever is necessary so you do not feel constricted in this area. It is also recommended you not do this on a full stomach of food.

If you do the meditation for longer than five minutes, you may begin to feel a tingling sensation in your hands or face. Your hands can be relaxed in your lap. If you already know about yoga "mudras" (finger posturing), then do whichever one you like. In addition, the suggestion to pace your breathing by mentally counting 1, 2, 3, and 4 could also be replaced with a *silent* four-syllable mantra if you know one that you like. This is just an embellishment to add another layer of higher frequency to your efforts.

Example of a four-part mantra to attach to each breath:
RAH - AH - MA - AH

This is a classical Raja Yoga mantra: *Rah* means "sun;" *ma,* means "moon." When you work up to doing the breathing in eight parts inhale and eight parts exhale, you can continue to match a one syllable mantra to each part, repeating the four–part mantra twice for each round.

Example of Four-Part Breath Combined With Four-Part Silent Mental Mantra:

RAH	AH	MA	AH	RAH	AH	MA	AH
inhale	inhale	inhale	inhale	exhale	exhale	exhale	exhale

This is just one of many meditations and breathing exercises that can help you relax and expand your consciousness, making it easier to actually see ch'i. I do not believe you have to be a seasoned meditation practitioner to get immediate results. I think anyone can make this subtle shift in their attention, which is why I am offering you this opportunity. If you find it difficult to sit up straight without support, then use a back support. You can even do this lying down, but it is so relaxing you may fall asleep before your meditation time is done.

- During your breathing/meditation session, periodically check your posture. It is very easy to slouch without even realizing it.

- To end your meditation session, inhale as deeply as possible in one long breath and try to hold the breath inside as long as possible. Then exhale powerfully.

- You will experience both insight and relaxation on your first try.

- You can practice this breath technique daily or at least for forty consecutive days, to master it.

Common Feng Shui Terms

So much of feng shui is shrouded in mysterious words that I know it can slow down comprehension while learning. It is also just a fact that some words in Chinese do not translate well into English, or we only have approximations on which to fall back. It is helpful to know the meanings of common terms before delving further.

Ch'i: I have already expounded a bit on this word. And it is sometimes called "life force energy" or "air currents." Ch'i affects your health and well-being. It is manipulated by the contents of a room. The dimensions of a room or house and the location of doors and windows will influence how the ch'i moves through the space. Ch'i movement is also influenced by exterior forces like roads and other buildings. A curvy road is like a curvy stream, carrying the ch'i with it.

Energy field: There are so many manifestations of ch'i and in the previous paragraph I described how ch'i (as a moving force) can be manipulated by objects, shapes, and dimensions. But there is also a type of ch'i which formulates in a structure based on when the structure is built and how it is oriented. This "energy field" is more or less stationary and remains in defined sections of a house. This is different than ch'i which moves through space like a draft blowing in from a window.

This energy field can expand or contract when people enlarge or reduce the size of a space during remodeling. It is both strange and comforting that the energy field has an intelligence or consciousness that recognizes the divisions of personal space. If you rented out a room in your house and created a separate exterior entrance for that room, the energy field of the house would recognize this division and begin to treat each space as separate houses. This may be similar to when you take a plant clipping and put it in its own soil; it can grow into its own full plant.

Quadrants: Square or rectangular shapes that define an area within your floor plan. This is a departure from the more common definition of the word "quadrant," which can mean the four sections of some shape. A house will have nine square or rectangular sections, representing each of the eight basic directions plus the center. Each one is commonly referred to as a quadrant just to distinguish it from a sector, which is a different division of space.

Like water, which has no shape until it is contained in something, the quadrants take their shape inside based on the exterior shape of the house or building. If a house is a square shape, then the directional quadrants inside will have a square shape. If the house is rectangular, then the individual quadrants will be rectangular.

Sectors: Starting from the center of a house and emanating out like a ray of light, the sectors of a house or property can look like pie-shaped wedges when they are drawn over a floor plan. In this book, there will be demonstrations of when to use the quadrant method or the sector method to locate the ideal location to place a remedy.

Elements: In Chinese metaphysics, the five elements are both symbolic and literal: water, wood, fire, earth, and metal. They have a harmonious cycle relationship as well as a destructive cycle relationship. When a feng shui element is recommended, like adding water to a room, it is for the purpose of strengthening a positive element or weakening a destructive element.

Flying Stars/numbers: These numbers are symbolic code for energy, as defined by the trigrams they are associated with. Each number represents a direction, an element, a family member, parts of the body, and *much more*. It takes a long time to understand how they behave in combinations and within the uniqueness of your own personal space. The numbers have nothing to do with Western numerology. Throughout this book, there will be references to certain numbers or "stars." Numbers and stars refer to the same thing: bundles of energy that occupy a space and that can be interpreted for their effects on the space. The Flying Stars reside within the quadrants. They inhabit the energy field just described.

Annual or yearly cycles: Semi-permanent energy is created in a structure when it is built and referred to as an energy field. But *changing* yearly influences also become active in a structure, lasting for one year from February to February. A metaphor for the annual cycle is like having a guest stay with you temporarily. The annual influences are either harmful or supportive and can be stimulated or suppressed with additional elements added to a room.

Facing side: This refers to the entire front side of a house or building. A facing quadrant is specifically the front middle section on the facing side.

Below is a rectangular space divided up into the nine "quadrants." If this were a house facing the bottom of the page, then the facing quadrant is the front middle section, noted with XXX.

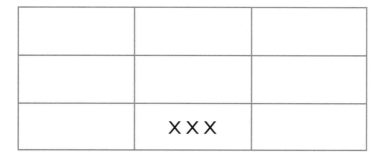

Sitting side: This refers to the entire back side of a house or building. A sitting quadrant is specifically the back middle section on the sitting side.

Below is the same rectangular space divided up as nine sections. If it were a house facing the bottom of the page, the back middle portion (XXX) would be called the sitting quadrant.

	X X X	

Do Feng Shui Remedies Ever Fail?

There are a number of reasons why feng shui applications do not always work and the following section categorizes some of those reasons.

Misdiagnosed: A property may have been misdiagnosed, and therefore some of the recommendations will be in error.

1. If the feng shui consultant is given the incorrect year that the structure was built, then part of the assessment will be off. I usually do not trust that a landlord will give the correct information to the tenant, so I verify it myself whenever possible with a title company or the tax assessor's office. You can probably obtain the year your home was built by doing a search for your city or county on the Internet or a phone call to your local Department of Building and Safety. However, these agencies do not always have listings of when room additions or remodels have been done. Sometimes we have to rely on the memories of neighbors to recall when additions were made when there is no record of additions being done with permits.

2. Sometimes it is difficult to get an accurate compass reading when surrounded by large metal buildings. For example, downtown Los Angeles is always a challenge. There are so many metal buildings clustered together and so many underground parking structures,

you cannot get away from all the metal and it disrupts the compass reading. It takes a lot of experience to compensate for these disruptions and figure out the correct reading. Sometimes even a residential neighborhood will have strong magnetic interference to throw off the compass. In New York City, a compass reading directly over the subway could also be made inaccurate.

Underground water is sometimes the culprit in throwing off a compass reading.

3. Sometimes the orientation of the house or office is dubious, based on the interior floor plan and other features, and a comparison of two possibilities can be made. Often, the recommendations for two different orientations will be contradictory and a person may just have to experiment with their options.

4. There are many practitioners who do not even use traditional diagnostic methods and rely instead solely on what they can physically see, perpetuated superstitions, or purported psychic abilities. These kinds of readings have the greatest chance for error.

When Clients Do Not Follow Recommendations

1. Sometimes a client will take in all the information, but still decide to "do their own thing." This may be in conflict with the original recommendations.

2. Sometimes a client will follow through with all of the minor recommendations, but not do the most important recommendations which have the potential to make the biggest difference.

3. In their enthusiasm to understand more about feng shui, clients often run out and buy books on the subject after their consultation. Based on the misinformation in so many of them, the client will often not follow through with the remedies which are specific to their house or they may try to combine remedies with the conflicting information they have read. This might be on par with taking both prescribed and unprescribed medications at the same time.

Unrealistic Expectations

Another problem with some books is that they give people unrealistic expectations of how much their remedies will work. Feng shui cannot usually change someone's destiny drastically. It usually improves the good and diminishes the bad, and that is difficult to qualify. As an example, you may not be able to completely escape having an illness one year, but with remedies in place it could be less severe or shorter in duration.

Changes may also come slowly and consumers have been brainwashed into believing that something dramatic should happen within days after the remedies have been put in place. When my own clients report immediate shifts, within hours or days, I almost find myself embarrassed to even take credit for it. What I am interested in seeing is long-term, sustained improvement, as opposed to a single event.

If a person has a fixed salary working for someone else, all the remedies in the world may not change that. Raises and promotions may come periodically, but when you do not own your own business, the prosperity remedies may only work in modest ways. Still, balancing your environment could help you in other ways not planned on or expected. And it should not always be about money.

Some people live in places with such bad feng shui, the remedies will only help a little bit. It is not the feng shui consultant's job to tell people their place is terrible and that their only hope is to move. When a person has this kind of situation to begin with, moving might only mean he or she will wind up in another place which is virtually identical if the person is stuck in a bad personal luck cycle.

Since feng shui is only a part of your life, a person may knowingly or unknowingly continue to do things that undermine or lessen the influence of the remedies. There are different reasons why a person may have a particular problem.

Let's say you are totally stressed out. Your nutritionist may tell you to stop drinking twelve cups of coffee per day. Your therapist may tell you to journal your feelings and start meditating. And your feng shui consultant may have several suggestions for balancing your space. To not address all of the contributing factors will reduce the effectiveness of any one thing you decide to do.

Percentage of Failure

There will always be a small percentage of houses that do not respond to remedies, for reasons that may never be known. This is a sad fact but a reality. If a doctor cures 95 percent of his patients, it would be unfair to him or his future patients to discontinue his practice because of the 5 percent who do not respond. One would hope that there is some other method or practitioner who is better suited for this client and that help may come from some other source.

Once in a great while I will have a client whose home does not seem to respond to remedies in an appropriate time frame. I will recommend that they see my astrologer for a personal reading. In 100 percent of these cases, the client learns that he or she is in a very difficult phase of his or her life (so the feng shui remedies will not work powerfully like they can for others).

Over the years I have also asked a handful of clients to *take away their remedies*, when they confided in me that nothing was improving. Invariably, they reported back that things got worse without the remedies, so they quickly reinstalled them. This was all the validation they needed to know that the remedies were in fact working on some level.

But what spurs me on to continue studying and consulting, is the consistent positive feedback I receive from people who follow through with the remedies and "let nature take its course."

CHAPTER TWO

Rome Wasn't Feng Shui-ed in a Day

Although it would be nice if conclusions could be made instantaneously, that cannot be the case with certain important aspects of an evaluation. There are some mechanics involved in diagnosing a house. They cannot be avoided or skipped over. Before interpreting your findings, you first have to be able to set up your data properly. To begin this chapter, we will go over the mechanics involved in organizing your data. Be patient; the reward of being accurate is worth it.

How to Draw an Accurate Floor Plan

Throughout this book, references will be made to directions. In order for you to really understand where these various directions are located inside your house, as well as outside of the house, you need to first draw a to-scale floor plan sketch. A realistic sketch will show you where these directional energies stop and start. The directional quadrants take up space—actual square footage—and knowing the real dimensions of these areas will prove extremely helpful. Some people question whether or not adjacent quadrants can partially blend with each other at their joining edges. My experience is that do not bleed into each other. Like Master Sang once said of adjacent quadrants, "They are like oil and water. They do not mix."

I understand that some folks are just not visually oriented and can't draw well. If there is no way that you can draw a semi-realistic sketch, please have someone help you or completely do it for you. You can always find an interior designer or architect to draft a floor plan for you if necessary.

Example of an Unacceptable Floor Plan

Figure 2A shows an example of an unacceptable drawing. The rooms are not in proportion and would never really be this way. This kind of drawing will not help you identify the right location for your remedies.

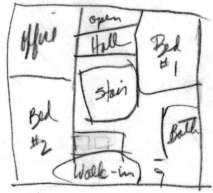

Figure 2A

Example of an Acceptable Floor Plan

Figure 2B shows a simple sketch that is drawn to scale.

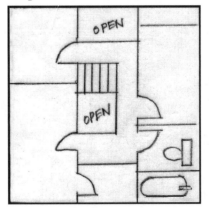

Figure 2B

Some people are lucky enough to already have a copy of their home's actual floor plan, given to them directly by the architect, the builder, or a past occupant. Most of my clients do not have floor plans, so I take the time to sketch one out for them. As well, after remodeling, the locations of walls and the dimensions of the house can change.

Don't let the suggestion to draw out your floor plan intimidate you. All you need are the following:

1. Graph paper

2. Measuring tape or electronic sonar device. I use the latter instead of measuring tape because it is quicker, and I measure rooms frequently. You can get these sonar devices, which look like a garage door opener, at hardware and home improvement stores. They send a signal from one wall or hard surface to whatever hard surface they are pointed at, and then display a digital reading of the measurement in feet and inches (or centimeters).

3. Writing utensils. Use a pencil so that you can erase easily as you perfect your drawing.

When I begin to draw a floor plan, I first decide how much I am going to reduce the dimensions. If I want to put a floor plan of a house that is under 2,000 square feet onto an 8½- by 11-inch piece of graph paper, I can cut the dimensions into halves, thirds, or quarters. I then draw it out in centimeters.

For example, if a room is 10 feet by 10 feet, I can draw it on the graph paper as 2.5 centimeters by 2.5 centimeters. If a room is 20 feet by 20 feet, I can shrink it down on the graph paper as 5 centimeters by 5 centimeters.

This is just a suggestion for getting the whole floor plan onto one piece of paper in a workable size format. For a larger home, you may want to reduce the dimensions even more, but not make the rooms so small that you cannot sketch in some of the furnishings. For two-story homes, you can use two pieces of graph paper, one for each floor.

Instead of trying to get the perimeter measurements of the house first, do your measurements inside and go from room to room. I like to start from one side or corner of the house and proceed to other rooms in a "connect the rooms" kind of format. With experience, I have found that rooms are often predictable sizes as well as closets and I have gotten a good "eye" for estimating the size of rooms. Do not be overly concerned with being 100 percent exact. I tend to round off odd sizes. If a wall actually registered as 11 feet and 2 inches away from the opposite wall, I would draw it as 11 feet. You want your floor plan sketch to be accurate, but remember, this is not an architectural blueprint, and you will have plenty of space to put your remedies in the right location.

Not everything is a box or rectangle, however, so check the outside of the house when you come up with measurements that would create protrusions or indentations anywhere from the body of the house.

Patios usually do not count as part of the body of the house when you are doing an overall measurement of a house's dimensions. There are exceptions, such as when outdoor space can be considered part of the overall "lo-shu" grid of the house. The lo-shu grid is the directional grid placed over a floor plan, which designates the eight directions, plus the center quadrant. An outside space used frequently and furnished like an interior room might be considered part of the lo-shu grid of the house, although this is somewhat rare. But if you live in an apartment and have a balcony, this is not considered part of your living space, although you can certainly include it on your floor plan sketch.

What you will create is an aerial view, as if you were peering down on the house with the ceiling removed. Drawing side elevations of a house are useful for other feng shui purposes, but not necessary most of the time or for what will be covered in this book.

How to Divide Up the Sections of the Floor Plan

Once you have completed your to-scale floor plan sketch, you are ready to divide up the directional quadrants that exist within the floor plan. Look at the floor plan sketch you have created. If it happens to be a square or rectangle, then the division of the space in equal thirds is easy.

Example of Rectangular-Shaped Floor Plan and the Equal Divisions of Quadrants

Figure 2C(a)

Example of a Square-Shaped Floor Plan Divided Into Equal Thirds

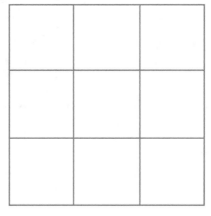

Figure 2C(b)

Many floor plans have a fully missing quadrant, a partially missing quadrant, or extensions. The way you determine if your house has an extension or a missing quadrant is by careful measurements when it is not obvious.

In Figure 2D, the floor plan has a missing quadrant because the area missing from the square is only a third of the length of that side of the floor plan.

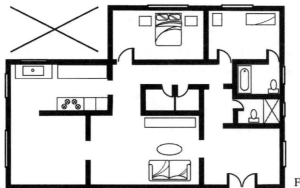

Figure 2D

If the part of a floor plan that protrudes is less than half the width of the house, then it is deemed an extension from the bulk body of the house (Figure 2E).

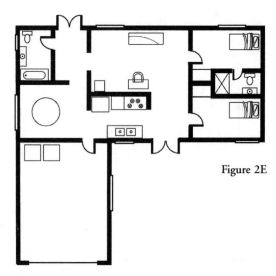

Figure 2E

These guidelines, for the proper division of space, are assuming that the entire space you are dividing is the original construction. Once you have remodel expansions and additions, then the general rules can change.

Figure 2F is an example of a rectangular-shaped house having its own complete -area grid. Then with the addition of another room at a later time, that singular room has its own miniature nine-area grid. It would not be considered an extension of the quadrant it is attached to because it was built later on. This illustration shows a lo-shu grid placed over the original house, along with a separate grid for the master bedroom addition.

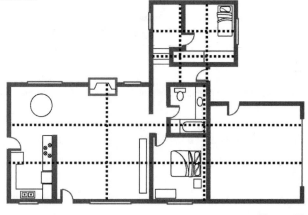

Figure 2F

When the Upstairs Does Not Have the Same Dimensions as the Downstairs

First, draw out the two floors on two separate pieces of paper. Reduce their dimensions in the same way for each floor. When a house is being built, the energy from the ground will emanate upwards. Take note of which rooms are over the downstairs rooms and be particularly careful in your division of the quadrants when the second floor is not as big as the first floor. There are even houses where the top floor is larger than the bottom floor. This is often the result of a house built into a mountainside. It is unusual, but it does exist.

There are two distinct practices for treating multi-story structures that do not have the same dimensions on each floor. Some practitioners will treat each floor as a separate universe and use the exterior walls for each floor to determine the dimensions of each quadrant. Figure 2G is an example of a floor plan where the first floor has its own nine-area grid. Next to it, the second floor has its own nine-area grid shrunk down to fit just inside the second-floor dimensions.

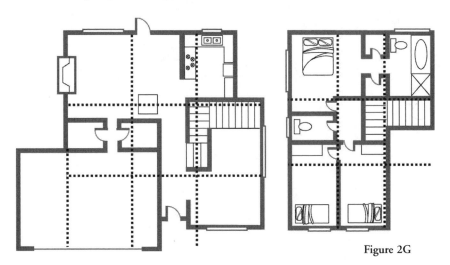

Figure 2G

I consider the largest floor to be the basic grid of the whole house and the smaller floor may just be lacking some or most of the quadrants on that particular level.

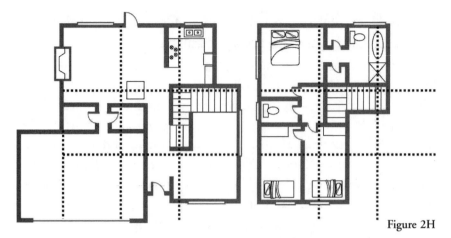

Figure 2H

Using the same floor plans as the previous example, this alternative method in Figure 2H shows how the second floor is only part of the first floor's nine-area grid. Here is a common floor plan, where the living room and dining room are "open" to the top floor, and bedrooms cover only part of the second floor.

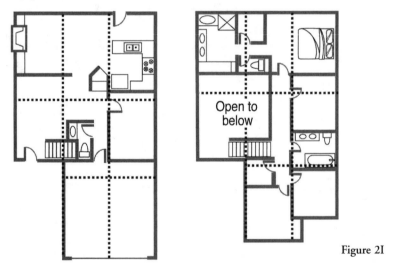

Open to below

Figure 2I

This two-story house in Figure 2I has a living room with double-high ceilings and the upstairs bedrooms are over only part of the first floor.

I am not going to criticize a colleague who always divides up the smaller floor based on its own dimensions. I may even do that once in a while on a case-by-case basis, such as a second floor that shares only a small opening to the first floor in the form of a normal staircase. But in the case of a home where the second floor only constitutes about half of the square footage of the first floor, and there is a *big open space* from below (usually the living room), then I would consider the second floor to be like a glorified loft. It would be just part of the "big picture," established at the first floor level and covered in some areas by the same ceiling.

As a comparison, if a child has a bunk bed in the bedroom, we don't consider the upper bunk bed to be its own room and have its own lo-shu grid. It is still encased by the same floor and ceiling of the room as a whole.

How to Diagnose an Apartment Versus a House

If you live in an apartment, then concentrate on the dimensions of your own personal area. If you live in a building that has a weird shape, that is not something to ignore. But it is also not relevant at the moment you are attempting to correctly divide up the quadrants in your own personal space. Follow the same guidelines as just outlined for a house.

Decks, balconies, and porches generally do not count as part of the directional grid placed over the floor plan of your apartment or house.

The apartment in Figure 2J has a balcony, but it is not part of the apartment's lo-shu grid.

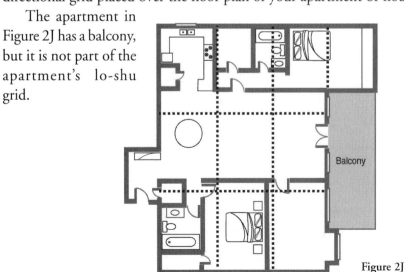

Balcony

Figure 2J

Have Compass, Will Travel

The importance of using a compass will be reinforced over and over again throughout this book. Here are some guidelines:

Rule 1: Do not be intimidated by a compass.

Rule 2: Get a good quality compass that delineates all 360 degrees. Compasses that show the division of directions in 5-degree increments are not good enough.

Rule 3: Do not make any adjustments with your compass reading based on the fact that magnetic north can be 0 to 18 degrees off of true north. Just take a reading and note exactly what your compass reads. We use magnetic compass directions in feng shui, so your compass will show you exactly what the magnetic directions are and you do not have to recalculate what true north is.

Rule 4: Don't stand near any metal objects.

Rule 5: Hold your compass level with the ground.

Rule 6: Position your body and your compass so that you are both parallel to the house or building.

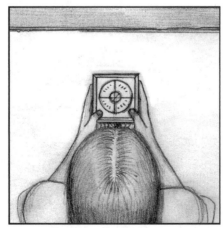

Figure 2K

Figure 2K is an aerial view of a person holding a compass with the edge aligned parallel to the façade of a house.

Rule 7: Note where your compass arrow is pointing (it will be 0 degrees magnetic north). If you use a Chinese feng shui compass, the arrow will point to 180 degrees south. The Chinese compass is oriented toward south simply because the Chinese prefer south. It is associated with the yang qualities of summer, growth, youth, and movement, whereas north is associated with winter, decay, old age, and stillness.

Rule 8: If there is a central dial on your Western-made compass, you will need to shift it so that the very tip of the arrow will be aligned with 0 degrees. For a Chinese-made feng shui compass, you will shift the dial so that the tip of the arrow lines up with 180 degrees south. There are different kinds of compasses, and some have a silhouette of an arrow that needs to surround the actual arrow in order to have the tip of the arrow aligned properly.

If this is all new to you, when purchasing a compass ask someone in the store to show you how to use it.

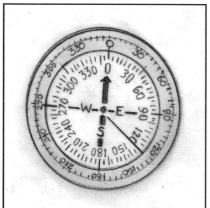

Figure 2L

The compass in Figure 2L shows an arrow pointing to north.

Rule 9: Whatever direction the entire structure is facing, it should read just about or exactly 180 degrees opposite on the other side of the structure. Once in a great while a front wall will not be parallel to a back wall, in which case the readings will not be exactly opposite. But most buildings have parallel and perpendicular exterior walls.

Rule 10: Take several readings from various distances from the property to make sure there is no magnetic interference that might change the compass reading (such as standing too close to a car when trying to take a compass reading on a driveway or near a street curb).

How to Locate Relevant Directions Outside the House

As seen throughout this book, floor plans are divided into directional quadrants in order to locate the boundaries of interior directions. But when remedies are needed on the outside of the house, the pie-shaped sectors are commonly used instead. The reference point begins at the center of the house, and the directions fan out from that center point. Extend the directional sectors beyond the exterior walls and let them radiate out as far as is needed or relevant to your application.

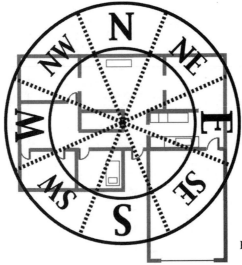

Figure 2M

This floor plan (Figure 2M) has sectors superimposed over it, showing how they radiate out like a fan.

There are a number of reasons why the sectors are used as an overlay to the boxy quadrants. The sector method will show you:

- The location of the 15-degree increment that is considered your "Lucky Money Spot," to be discussed in Chapter Four.

- The location for placing a Romance Remedy called the Peach Blossom cure, to be explained in Chapter Six.

- How to locate directions that can either drain you or activate your creative process, to be discussed in Chapters Four and Five.

- How the current era Flying Stars come toward a house at the precise angle determined by the current construction cycle. If a current era Flying Star is aligned directly with someone's front door, it is another aspect to consider in how a person is affected by their front door. This becomes even more meaningful after you study more of the Flying Star School. You do not use remedies on the current era Flying Stars. They just exist where they are, and they have a subtle effect.

The Influence of the Current Era Energies

Some of you are already familiar with the Flying Star School. This upcoming section caters to those of you who already know this formula but should offer insight to beginners as well. From 2004 through 2023, the planet resonates the "Period 8" Cycle.

The Period 8 Chart looks like the chart given here.

NW	N	NE
9	4	2
W		E
1	8	6
SW	S	SE
5	3	7

This current era chart is full of meaning. In the context just described, if you have a front door that is inside one of the directional sectors, you can also add the current era number to your evaluation. It will not be as influential as the Flying Stars created inside your house based on when it was built, but it is another layer of meaning.

Following are two examples of looking at the current era chart as a subtle overlay to a more advanced reading.

From 2004–2023 (Current Era 8, often called Period 8) we see that the 5 Star is in the direction of southwest. This 5 energy can indicate potential for disasters and pain. To a certain extent, we can say that the southwest portion of the United States may have some event within this twenty-year period that could have far-reaching negative consequences. Where in the southwest are we talking about? This area covers several states such as Nevada, Arizona, and Southern California. This might be the danger in giving out general information, but on some level this southwest direction within the United States, and this southwest direction within each state, and within each city, could be vulnerable to a major mishap.

LAX (Los Angeles International Airport) sits in the southwest-most corner of the city. This airport has become much more vulnerable in the current Period 8 era than it was in the previous Period 7 era (1984–2003). Los Angeles International Airport is unfortunately a very attractive location for terrorists and threats are made regularly.

We have that expression "an accident waiting to happen." It is more than likely that Southern California will also have a larger than "normal" earthquake within this time frame. The added component to this prediction rests in the fact that the 5 Star is inherently earthy in nature, so earthquakes are directly related to aspects of the 5 and 8 Stars when combined. The 8 Star is the Ken trigram, which is known for stillness, like a mountain. But some influences like the 5 Star can move it into action. Real estate has an implied relationship with the 5 and 8 Stars.

When I first started studying with Master Sang in 1992, the direction of southwest had an *annual* 5 Star. Master Sang mentioned in class at that time that this destructive annual 5 in the southwest had something to do with the Los Angeles riots that year. Even the month that they started (last week in April) had a monthly energy associated with fire and explosions (monthly 9 Star).

On a more positive note, I have noticed in my own home that my main door used to have a current era 3 Star when I first moved there in 2002. But after the change in 2004, I have a current era 4 Star at my main door until 2024. I find it no coincidence that my writing and publishing efforts started to manifest directly after this shift. (The 4 Star is associated with a number of attributes, including writing and scholarly achievement.)

You will learn more about what some of these "numbers" mean in later chapters. Whatever number is being discussed, it can have a similar effect whether it is a permanent, annual, monthly, or current era number.

Obviously, a monthly 4 Star is temporary but it can predict a certain event. Let us say your child had a monthly 4 Star in his or her bedroom. He or she may perform in the school play that month or receive some other kind of scholastic recognition. If the 4 Star was a yearly influence in someone's home, it may indicate an entire year of advances in career and creative fields. If the 4 Star is permanent (and every house has the 4 energy stationed in two places), that is an area that can always support creative endeavors.

CHAPTER THREE

Have You Hugged Your House Today?

How to Choose the Best Color for the Exterior

Most houses have a basic exterior color and then a complementary color for the trim around the windows and doors. Does it matter what color you paint your house? On a subtle level, the color of the main exterior body of the house will have either a strengthening, neutral, or weakening affect on the house.

The end result is that this can strengthen or weaken the occupants who live or work inside. Every structure, including a house, will have a sitting direction that is defined as the back of the house. Whatever direction the back of the house happens to be, it will have an element associated with it. That element can then be matched with the color it is associated with (which has a neutral affect) on the house.

For example, a house that "sits" in the west means that its back wall faces between 248 and 292 degrees. You can refer to the compass illustration or compass chart in the first chapter to see the 45-degree range that constitutes the range of west.

The direction of west is associated with the metal element. Metal colors are white, gray, silver, and gold. So if your house sits in the west (which means it faces east), then to paint it white or gray simply matches the house type.

Here is a brief overview of the five elements as color choices:

- Water = any shade of blue or black
- Wood = any shade of green
- Fire = any shades of red
- Earth = any variations of yellow, orange, or brown
- Metal = any shades of gray, white, silver, or gold

Each of the eight basic directions is associated with one of these elements, as follows:

NW	North	NE
metal	water	earth
white, gray	blue, black	yellow
West	Center	East
metal	earth	wood
white, gray	yellow	green
SW	South	SE
earth	fire	wood
yellow	red	green

Based on knowing what real direction your house "sits," you can choose a color palette that simply matches your house type. The backside is always referred to as "sitting," like someone sitting in a chair with their back up against it for support. A house can be like a person with their back to a particular direction.

Yin-Yang Theory to Define the Orientation of a House

Features of the *facing* side of house	Features of the *sitting* side of house
Considered the front **(YANG)**	Considered the back **(YIN)**
Brightest side of house	Darkest side of house
Most views	Least views
Biggest rooms (used during waking hours)	Smallest rooms (often used for sleeping)
Living rooms, great rooms	Major cluster of plumbing (bathrooms, laundry, kitchen)
Closest proximity to yang exterior features like a road or the ocean	Backed up to an alley or mountain, and often includes the garage side of house

The concept of "sitting" and "facing" justifies further explanations and examples. But common sense can often reveal the true orientation of a house. If the house were a person, what direction would it look toward? Often, the architectural layout makes it obvious, but sometimes people erroneously assume that the street side of a house must be the front and this is not necessarily the case. If your house has an intentional view of the ocean or a valley from what you think of as your backyard, then nine times out of ten that is the facing side of your house.

Also, modern design has changed the more simplified assumptions about facing verses sitting. For instance, the kitchen almost always used to be considered part of the back of the house, but that is not necessarily so anymore. Sometimes the kitchen is a real showcase room, adjacent to a large informal family room and dining area combined, looking out to major views. The master bedroom is now frequently placed on the facing side of a house, particularly in apartments and condominiums.

Remember, a house's name or character is based on the sitting side, not the facing side. A house that sits in the northeast is associated with an inherently earth direction since northeast is the Ken trigram (hard earth). Painting the house yellow or tan would just match the basic house type.

Because south is inherently associated with fire, does this mean you have to paint a south-sitting house red? Not by any means, but this is one of the house types that *could* get away with a red exterior! Every once in a while I drive by a house near Beverly Hills that is actually painted "barn red." The house faces north, therefore sitting south. When I pass by this house, I always think about how this house is so well suited to its red exterior.

The five elements have a relationship with each other and each element has a nurturing or productive relationship with one of the other elements, as follows:

Element (like a mother)	Nurtures (produces)	Element (like a child)
Water...	Feeds, makes grow...	Wood
Wood...	Feeds, creates...	Fire
Fire...	Feeds, produces...	Earth
Earth...	Feeds, creates...	Metal
Metal...	Strengthens or liquefies like	Water

Now you have some other options for what color to paint the exterior of your house.

Example: If your house sits northwest, that is inherently a metal direction. Since earth nurtures metal, you could use any earth colors for the exterior of this house as well, not just metal colors.

Consistent with each house type, there will be a nurturing or strengthening color to enhance the sitting direction of the house. Next is a chart for easy reference.

Best Exterior Color for Your House Chart

Sitting Direction	Matching Colors	Enhancing Colors
NW Sitting	gray, white	earth tones
North Sitting	Blue	white, gray
NE Sitting	yellow, peach, tan	fire colors
East Sitting	all shades green	blue
SE Sitting	all shades green	blue
South Sitting	red tones	green tones
SW Sitting	all earth colors	fire colors
West Sitting	white, gray	earth colors

The following chart shows colors that would be *harmful* or at least not ideal, because these colors would have a dominating effect on the house type described. This information comes straight from Five-Element Theory.

Undermining Exterior Color for Your House Chart

Sitting Direction	Dominating Color—not as good
NW (metal)	fire colors—fire destroys metal
North (water)	Earth colors—earth blocks water
NE (earth)	wood colors—wood depletes earth
East (wood)	metal colors—metal chops wood
SE (wood)	metal colors—metal chops wood
South (fire)	water colors—water stops fire
SW (earth)	wood colors—wood depletes earth
West (metal)	fire colors—fire destroys metal

As an example, it would not be good to paint an east-sitting house white. White is a metal color and metal chops or destroys wood. The east-sitting house can be categorized as a wood-type house. *This does not mean that the interiors have to emphasize wood furniture. We are only discussing the detail of exterior paint color right now.*

Nor would it be good to paint a north-sitting house yellow because north is associated with water and water is dominated by earth. Yellow is an earth color. This color would have a debilitating effect on the house and its occupants.

Domination Cycle of the Elements Chart

Element (initially stronger)	Dominates/Controls potentially destroys	Element (becomes weaker)
Earth	blocks, absorbs	Water
Water	extinguishes	Fire
Fire	melts down	Metal
Metal	chops, pierces	Wood
Wood	depletes	Earth

Does the color of the trim matter? Yes, on some minute level, but much less so than the basic exterior. The color of the exterior walls covers a much larger area so that should be your main focus. Think of it in these terms: If someone was driving by your house, he or she would most likely notice only the basic exterior wall color and not the trim.

What about the color of a roof? A client once called me, very disturbed to read somewhere that a blue roof signals disaster for the occupants and this was the color roof tile she had. Keep in mind that each house is unique and no one color can be good or bad for every house. Nor can just the color of a roof spell disaster for a family. There would have to be several other more important features out of balance in order for it to bring them such bad luck. This is just one of countless examples where people have unnecessarily panicked over a detail or a generality that did not apply to them.

Extreme Colors

Over the years I have seen extreme colors used for both inside and outside a house. Not too far from where I live there is a home that is painted magenta. This is an affluent area of west Los Angeles, and I am sure the neighbors have mixed feelings about this house. I have also seen bathrooms and bedrooms with black walls, red walls, and every color imaginable. Sometimes these bold colors look fantastic and sometimes they look horrible. By following the guidelines just described for your home's *exteriors*, you can achieve one level of balance to your surroundings, but do not feel limited by these guidelines, especially if you live somewhere in which you have no control over the exterior colors used.

How to Choose the Best Colors for the Interior?

Here are some comments and basic guidelines:

The ultimate best color for an individual room is based on the advanced Flying Stars of the room itself. The advanced Flying Stars are a set of calculations, based on the whole house's precise compass orientation, in conjunction with the year it was built. (This is beyond the scope of this book but will be presented in my third book.) Get professional assistance if you really want to know the long-term best interior colors for any room in your house.

Some interior colors will be recommended over others to suit the energies and personalities of the occupants. For example, blue is a relaxing, calming color. But for someone who is chronically depressed, it could drag his or her energy down even further and may not be appropriate.

Ceilings should not be darker than walls and walls should not be darker than floors. This has to do with how the eyes perceive color and light. Ceilings that are darker than walls can make a person's eyes strain, and he or she will feel pressure or disorientation over time. This is a principle that is important for homes; however, if you want to paint the ceiling of your restaurant black, that will not have a deleterious affect on patrons.

I wish it were simple enough to say that dining rooms should be a certain color and bedrooms another color, but that would actually be meaningless in the real scope of feng shui. Each home is unique and requires its own palette of colors, based more on the location of a room in a house than on the function of the room. In fact, if you read another feng shui book that states a particular room should be a certain color based solely on its function, this is clearly wrong and not to be taken seriously.

Yin-Yang Balance

An entire book could be written just about the manifestations of yin and yang. One of my clients is a macrobiotic chef, and I was fascinated to learn from her the different food groups classified as yin and yang. Even cooking styles can be broken down into the five elements!

When it comes to your physical environment, a simple example or manifestation of yin verses yang is temperature. A house that is chronically hot is considered too yang and a house that is chronically cold is considered too yin. Everywhere you look there are manifestations of yin-yang theory. Mountains are generally regarded as yin (since they are still) and the ocean is generally regarded as yang (because it moves). But even in these general categories there can be subdivisions, which yield more insight into whether or not the environment is healthy or harmful.

A mountain can be described as a yin mountain if it is just hard rock or covered with sand. If there is no life on the mountain, it is especially yin, and it can correlate with an impoverished group of people who live close to the lifeless mountains. In comparison, a yang mountain is full of life, oily green plants, birds, and animals. People who live near "yang" mountains are much happier, healthier, and prosperous.

Water can also be subdivided into yin water and yang water, even though it is initially a yang force. Yin water would be very still, even stagnant, which could attract bacteria and other unhealthful circumstances. Yang water is circulating and generally much better to be around. But water can also be too yang and move too forcefully. A tsunami may be the most aggressively yang example of water's power.

The human body can be divided up into left and right sides, and governed by two distinct hemispheres of the brain. In order to create a yin-yang balance of the mind, you can use an alternate breathing technique to achieve the experience you want.

Breathing through the *left* nostril stimulates the right hemisphere of the brain. Just doing left nostril breathing exclusively will calm the nerves and mind and activate the yin or feminine aspects of your personality. It can also stimulate creativity. Breathing through the *right* nostril exclusively will activate the left hemisphere of the brain for more logical, rational thinking.

In a nutshell, if you need to relax or have difficulty sleeping, try five to ten minutes of left nostril breathing before going to bed. If you need stimulation and don't want to drink caffeine, try five to ten minutes of right nostril breathing. The reality is that you breathe primarily through one nostril at a time and then it switches every few hours throughout the day. This can account for some of your energy levels and mood changes throughout the day. A person with a deviated septum, who only breathes through one nostril, will not be able to benefit from this natural balancing act that our bodies go through. I know one man who had his deviated septum fixed and once he could breathe through both nostrils, he said that his personality changed.

But just like feng shui, where you can manipulate the ch'i as it moves through a room (as with furniture placement), you can also manipulate your own bodily ch'i through the conscious selection of your nostril breathing.

The following is another meditation/breathing technique that has numerous benefits, including another method for slowing down the mind, becoming more aware, and making it easier to experience and actually see the ch'i in a room.

Meditation for Inner Yin-Yang Balance

Sit with your spine straight but not tense. Use a support for your back if needed. Begin to breathe exclusively through the left nostril, both the inhalation and the exhalation. You can hold up your right hand, near the nose and block off the right nostril with your right thumb. Just cap off the right nostril with the pad of your right thumb. You can have the other fingers of your right hand point upwards, like antennae. Do this exclusive left nostril breathing for at least five minutes.

Figure 3A shows a person sitting straight, eyes closed, with right thumb blocking off right nostril and the fingers of the right hand pointing upwards.

Figure 3A

Now switch your nostril breathing and breathe exclusively through the right nostril. Block off the left nostril with your left hand, capping off the left nostril with the pad of the left thumb. The other fingers on the left hand can point upwards like antennae. Breathe through the right nostril only for at least five minutes.

This alternate nostril breathing can be done as a complete ten-minute meditation as described. You can also extend each part, such as seven and one-half minutes with each nostril for a total of fifteen minutes.

Variations: With this alternate breathing technique, you can also go back and forth twice, such as five minutes of left nostril breathing, five minutes of right nostril breathing, then repeat each side for five minutes for a total of twenty minutes of long deep breathing.

Always breathe as deeply as possible, savoring your increasing lung capacity. The more oxygen you can push through your lungs, the more you will be purifying your bloodstream. For deeper concentration and fewer distractions, do these breathing exercises with your eyes closed.

This alternate nostril breathing meditation balances the yin-yang aspects of both sides of the body and both hemispheres of the brain.

The yogis from centuries ago would demonstrate their powers of mind over matter by doing outrageous things, such as sitting on a bed of nails or walking over hot coals. Some yogis were known for levitating on their sheep skins (magic carpets). I am not insinuating that it is easy or even possible to attain these *siddhi* powers just through breathing, but the simple benefits gained such as relaxation and better concentration make this worth trying.

When you do these breathing exercises, you can try to let your mind go blank or just focus on each breath and become highly aware of it. But it is also perfectly fine to let your mind wander. This is not a meditation book, where the reasons for concentrating will be highlighted.

The breathing exercises given in this book will still have a calming effect and simultaneously strengthen your nervous system even if you are not trying to clear your mind intentionally. Think of it this way: If you walked vigorously on the treadmill and worried the entire time, you would still be getting a physical workout and there would be a multitude of benefits even if your mind was not totally cooperating.

Feng Shui Principles for Gardens and Landscapes

The branch of feng shui that concerns itself with the garden or natural landscape is called "Landscape School" and it is a part of "Form School" feng shui.

There are four major reasons for paying attention to a garden or a home's immediate exterior landscape:

1. To make sure the house is adequately protected from harsher elements, such as wind and rain.

2. To enhance the energies inside the house because inside and outside work together.

3. To shore up or help maintain the good energies that flow around a structure.

4. To create an extension of the house and its functions.

Reason #1

When you have a house that is perched at the very top of a hill, it can be vulnerable to forceful winds. What is needed is an armchair-like landscape where there can be walls, hedges, and/or trees to protect the house from having too much wind whipping around it. In addition, if you have a house at the bottom of a hill, it could be vulnerable to flooding, so the landscape would need to help divert or shield the house from an onslaught of excessive water damage.

There always needs to be a balance. For instance, a property that has too many trees can cast a chronic shadow on the house, making it dark and possibly making the occupants feel depressed. At the same time, a house without any greenery around it will feel desolate and the full brunt of the sun beating down on it can make the occupants feel desperate and weary.

Reason #2

Enhancing the energies inside a house by doing something on the *outside* is confirmation that the two spaces work together. They influence each other. If you have a pool outside the house, but aligned very closely with an interior area that should not have any water, I have seen problems as a result of that. As an example, in some cases water in or near a particular room could increase gossip or sexual infidelity. A pool just 5 feet away from the bedroom could be as strong as a little fountain inside the room.

There are four major house types. Two of those house types should have water in the front, and two of those house types should technically have water in the back. In advanced Flying Star feng shui, it is determined which house types benefit from water on the front or back of the property. This means that water features should not be placed randomly just because they may look or feel nice, but for a specific and targeted reason.

Some houses need mountain type energy near them and this can be satisfied with hedges, walls, and elevated land level, when a real mountain or hill is not actually close by. If the ground on either side of your house is at least a few feet higher than on the opposite side, that extra height can be interpreted as "mountain" energy.

Reason #3

Most properties have a defined shape to the lot itself. In a residential setting, the lot may be outlined with fences or walls, sometimes by a change in the land level. If there is a gaping hole in the perimeter of the property or no physical perimeter at all, the end result is that the occupants will have difficulties saving money. Think of it like a slow plumbing leak. Therefore, a major goal in feng shui gardening techniques is to make sure this does not happen. It matters less which plants or trees are used, just so long as they are creating a less permeable border to the property.

Reason #4

Sometimes the garden is most useful as an extension of the living space and to provide tranquil, meditative views. If a room is relatively small, but can provide large windows or glass doors leading to a garden, it gives the occupant the pleasant illusion of being outside. It also makes the room inside feel bigger. For windows that look out to a close wall, you can convert that stifling view by placing a flowered trellis up against it and at least make it look attractive.

In keeping with the ideal that your home is your castle, having a beautiful, lush, healthy garden can also be a wonderful retreat from the stresses of life. This, in and of itself, is good feng shui.

Feng Shui Garden Myths

1. Each corner of your garden or backyard represents a life station (such as wealth and marriage). This notion was created in the 1970s and is an extension of the Black Hat Bagua Map. I have found it to be totally irrelevant.

2. Your garden furniture must be a certain element (such as wood or metal) depending on where you position it. I understand that some remedies are very subtle, but this is just an example of how some people try to apply Five Element Theory where it is not needed.

3. Specifically colored flowers are needed in certain directions. This is another example of people making things up, misinterpreting the Five-Element Theory, and creating unnecessary rules.

4. A tree aligned with a front door should be removed. (This is only necessary if the tree is very close to the door and actually blocking light and impeding easy access to the door.)

5. Plants with pointy leaves attract negative ch'i. Most plants look and feel very friendly to me, personally. Unless you positioned a cactus plant or a thorny rose bush too close to where someone might pass by, I cannot imagine any other plant being something to worry about.

General Garden Truths

1. A dead or dying lawn or withering plants will drain the land of its good ch'i (life force energy).

2. A diseased tree or one that buckles foundation or strangles plumbing should be removed.

3. A pool should not be too close to a house. A distance of at least 10 to 15 feet or more is preferred.

4. Curving, meandering paths in a garden are better than straight passage ways because the ch'i (as air currents) can develop more healthful effects when they curl and wind.

CHAPTER FOUR

Put Your Money Where Your House Is

Houses are built within twenty-year construction cycle time frames. During each construction cycle there will be good and bad directions for the placement of an *outside* water feature. This could be as small as a water fountain or as large as a pool. And by close proximity to a river, lake or the ocean, there will be an over-riding effect that can influence an entire community.

Each twenty-year cycle is associated with a direction. That direction is considered strong and positive. It has an upper hand over the other directions during its reigning time frame. But it is *not* a good direction for water in relation to where your house is. Everything is relative to directions, so it is imperative that you use a compass and really understand the magnetic compass alignment of your property.

Using Water for Prosperity

From 2004 through 2023, this Construction Cycle is known as "Period 8" or Construction Cycle 8. The number 8 is associated with the Ken trigram and the direction of northeast. This means that northeast is *not* a good direction for water placement in relation to your structure. At the same time, the direction exactly opposite of northeast (southwest) is the *best* location for water.

Prosperity Water Formula Number 1

The direction that is the exact *opposite* of the "timely governing" direction is the best location for water.

Figure 4A shows an example of a house that faces northeast. It would not be good to place a water fountain in front of this house, aligned with the northeast part of the house. Here is a northeast-facing house with a fountain to the northeast. Period 8 is not a good time to align water to the northeast of a house. It would, however, be good to place water aligned with southwest, during the twenty-year time frame called Period 8.

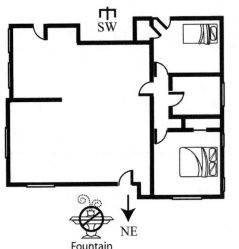

Figure 4A

Fountain

NE

Figure 4B shows the same northeast-facing house, but water is aligned to the southwest instead.

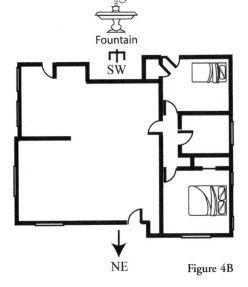

Fountain

SW

NE

Figure 4B

In the previous chapter, I mentioned that some houses benefit greatly from having water on the front side or back side. What do you do if your house needs water on the front side and it is a northeast-facing house?

In Figure 4C, you see a house that faces NE2 or 3. If this house was built between the years 1984 and 2003 then it would be the kind of house that technically can have water on its facing side. All you have to do to get around this situation is to place water in the north or the east, but not in between in the northeast. This illustration shows a house facing northeast, with quadrants superimposed over the floor plan to show how water can still be on front side, but aligned with north or east and avoiding the northeast area.

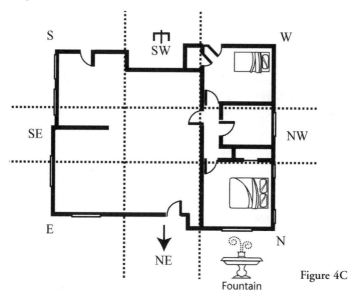

Figure 4C

Fountain

No one who desires to apply feng shui principles would want to build a pool in an area that currently is or will soon be a bad direction in the near future. This water formula should make it very clear why there are contradictions in other books about the best placement of water. Without the knowledge of timing, someone might arbitrarily think that there are only a few good directions for all time, when this actually changes over twenty-year periods.

Following is a chart that shows twenty-year construction cycles from the recent past as well as the future. *This cycle repeats itself every 180 years.* You can see what direction is associated with the time frame and its opposite direction being the absolute best location for water. This always refers to water outside the structure and when other circumstances inside a house are permitting, it can be applied to the interiors as well.

Important Note: Structures are built in twenty-year construction cycles. If you see a time frame listed in this book, it includes all the years in the range. For instance, 1984 through 2003 (1984–2003) means 1984 *through all of 2003,* not up until 2003. Further, both the annual and twenty-year cycles actually begin on February 4 each year. So the time frame 2004 through 2023 should literally be understood as February 4, 2004, through February 3, 2024. The beginning and end of each of these cycles is in February rather than January.

Prosperity Water Formula Number 1 Chart

Construction Cycles:

	1944–1963	1964–1983	1984–2003	2004–2023	2024–2043	2044–2063	2064–2083	2084–2103	2104–2123
Direction Associated with Time	See Footnote Below	NW 6	West 7	NE 8	South 9	North 1	SW 2	East 3	SE 4
Best Location for Water	See Note Below	SE	East	SW	North	South	NE	West	NW

Footnote: 1944–1963 was known as Period 5 or Construction Cycle 5. The number 5 is inherently associated with the location of center, so there is no real direction attached to it. Because of its special nature, Period 5 is actually broken down into two subcategories.

The first half of that cycle (1944–1953) is connected to the previous cycle of Period 4 and 4 is the Sun trigram of SE. Therefore, during that time frame, NW was the best spot for water since it is the opposite of SE.

The second half of the last Period 5 Cycle was 1954–1963 and it went with the succeeding Period 6. The Period 6 time Cycle is associated with the direction of northwest. Therefore, during that time frame, the opposite direction of northwest (which is southeast) became the best spot for water.

The next time we have a Period 5 Construction Cycle will be 2124 through 2143. This period will get split in half like the last Period 5, just described.

Important Note: I am aware that there is another interpretation of what to do during the Period 5 Cycle. Instead of having the first half of the cycle associated with Period 4 and the second half associated with Period 6, there are other feng shui schools that give a different formula where the first half is associated with Period 2 (southwest) and the second half is associated with Period 8 (northeast). I am not going to say this is incorrect; it is just not from the tradition I have studied or practice.

You may want to go back in time and make note of where fountains and pools were located in previous residences or currently occupied residences. As an example, perhaps you grew up in house that had a pool in a certain direction that benefitted your family tremendously in the 1960s or 1970s. Now you have inherited that home and your tenants are having all kinds of problems, possibly attributed to the location of the pool, which may now be *currently* considered a bad location. These are the kinds of things I have corroborated with actual clients.

Water aligned with the southwest exteriors in Period 8 can stimulate financial luck.

Water aligned with the northeast exteriors in Period 8 can sabotage financial luck. You can put water in a neutral location, meaning that it is neither a good nor bad direction for that particular time frame.

Prosperity Water Formula Number 2

What was just described and the chart above could be considered the *Number 1* spot for exterior water. But there is a *Number 2* spot that is also very powerful. Many of my clients have put water outside, aligned with both the best and second-best spots, to achieve very good results in increasing their income. Let's just say that the water fountain more than pays for itself!

If you study feng shui further, you will find out that the "5" energy is quite a chameleon and part of other calculations and remedy considerations. Some books refer to the 5 energy as the "Evil Emperor" or the "5 Yellow Star." When it happens to be in a good phase, it is very positive in its influence; but when it is not in a good phase, it can exert a very negative influence. Once again, remember that these numbers are not just numbers. They are code for energy and elements. In the same way that H_2O represents water, the numbers in feng shui calculations represent elements, directions, parts of the body, forces of nature, members of a family, and more.

Back in Period 5 (1944–1963), the 5 Star was considered the best prosperity energy. Now it is fully in a downward cycle and usually indicates a potential for negative things to occur.

Here in Water Formula Number 2, the number 5 is simply used to determine the second best location for water for increasing prosperity.

Whatever time frame you are looking into, take note of the number associated with it and then subtract 5 or add 5 to that number. You will end up with another single-digit number that indicates the second best location for water. All of these numbers represent trigram directions.

Refer back to the chart above. Note that 1984 through 2003 was the Period of 7. Subtract 5 from 7 (7 – 5 = 2). The number 2 is associated with southwest. Therefore, the direction of southwest was the second best location for water in Period 7. It just happens to have moved to the best spot for Period 8 because of the first water formula.

Skip forward to Construction Cycle 9; 9 – 5 = 4. Therefore, during that time frame southeast will be the second best location for water because the 4 Star represents the Sun trigram of Southeast.

So for Periods 9, 8, 7, and 6 you will subtract 5 and get a number associated with a direction. That will be considered the second best location for exterior water.

When considering a time frame represented by a number less than 5, such as Periods 1, 2, 3, and 4 you will ADD the number five instead of subtracting it.

For example: in Construction Cycle 2, add 5 + 2 to get 7. Since 7 is the Tui trigram (west), in that time frame the west will be the second best location for exterior water.

Prosperity Water Formula Number 2 Chart

Cycle	6	7	8	9	I	2	3	4	5A*	5B*
Direction Associated With Time	NW	W	NE	S	N	SW	E	SE	SE	NW
Second Best Location for Water	North	SW	East	SE	NW	W	NE	S	S	North

*5A stands for the first ten years of Period 5 or Construction Cycle 5.
*5B stands for the second ten years of Period 5 or Construction Cycle 5.

Rules Regarding Water

- Water should be clean, never dirty.
- Water ideally should be circulating, not stagnant.
- Water can flow from a higher plateau to a lower level or at least toward a property and not away from it.
- It is also fine if the water stays at the same level and just moves from a submerged pump.
- Water needs to circulate for at least a few hours per day to be affective.
- You can usually have the water running continuously if you want.
- If you live in an area where outside water would freeze in the winter, then you simply have to rely on other prosperity remedies inside the house or building during cold weather season.
- If you want to be especially careful about the timing of when you start digging for a pool, *Feng Shui for Skeptics* reveals two formulas for calculating the directions to avoid constructions in any given year, so as not to aggravate an area and cause delays or injuries.

Your Personal Wealth Direction

You have a superbly lucky direction, based on your year of birth and gender. It is related to your personal trigram, sometimes called a "gua" or "kua" number. It comes from the Eight Mansion School of feng shui. It can be considered a "wealth" or prosperity direction. It is based on a solar calendar that is used frequently for feng shui applications. There will be other opportunities to do feng shui remedies based on your Chinese zodiac sign and examples will be given in this book as well. But you will refer to the solar calendar for your personal trigram.

Take a look at the Personal Trigram Wealth Chart in this chapter. Based on the year you were born and your gender, you will see a direction listed that you can personally identify as your own prosperity direction, no matter where you live or work.

A very important detail is that this solar calendar begins on February 4, not on January 1. So, if you were born between January 1 and February 3, consider yourself one year older, born in the previous year. Example: If you were born January 14, 1957, you should consider yourself born in 1956 instead.

You take that lucky direction with you wherever you go. That direction will benefit you when you use it in any number of ways about to be described:

Personal Wealth Direction Chart

Female birth year	Wealth direction	Male birth year	Wealth direction
1970	South	1970	South
1971	North	1971	Northeast
1972	Southwest	1972	Southeast
1973	West	1973	East
1974	Northwest	1974	Southwest
1975	Southwest	1975	Northwest
1976	East	1976	West
1977	Southeast	1977	Northeast
1978	Northeast	1978	North

Female birth year	Wealth direction	Male birth year	Wealth direction
1979	South	1979	South
1980	North	1980	Northeast
1981	Southwest	1981	Southeast
1982	West	1982	East
1983	Northwest	1983	Southwest
1984	Southwest	1984	Northwest
1985	East	1985	West
1986	Southeast	1986	Northeast
1987	Northeast	1987	North

This cycle repeats itself every nine years, so if you don't see your birth year listed, then just find a year that is some multiple of nine years older than you or younger than you on the chart. For instance, the chart starts with 1970. If you were born in 1961, that is nine years away from 1970, so you have the same wealth direction as that year. Not everyone will find it practical or possible to sleep in their wealth direction, but if you can, then try it out.

Sleep with your head pointing in that direction for increased wealth luck, but not necessarily sounder sleep.

Figure 4D shows a Sun trigram person, sleeping with his head to north, which is his personal wealth direction.

Figure 4D

Enter a house through that directional quadrant. For a Tui trigram person, northwest is his or her wealth direction, so entering through a northwest entrance can enhance his or her personal wealth luck (Figure 4E).

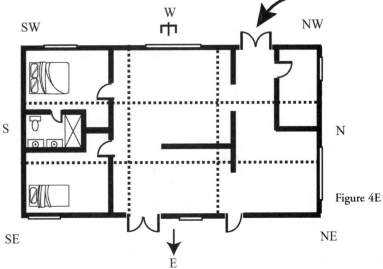

Figure 4E

Enter a room through that directional quadrant for the room (a microcosm of the house or building). Here is an example of a southwest entrance into an office, which is a Ken person's personal wealth direction (Figure 4F). Position your desk in that quadrant of a room.

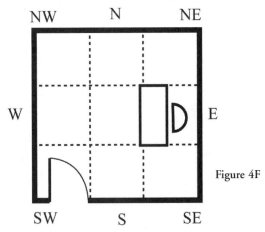

Figure 4F

Following is an example of a desk in the northeast quadrant of a room, which is the personal wealth direction for a K'un trigram person (Figure 4G). Face that direction when doing business with others, such as when you are trying to convince clients, customers, or patients to use your services.

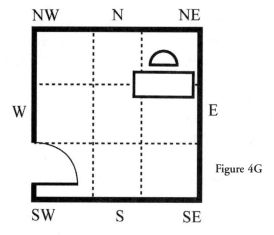

Figure 4G

Figure 4H is an example a desk, facing south, across from a customer or client for a Chen trigram person.

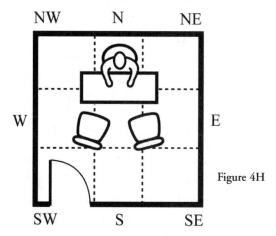

Figure 4H

There are differences of opinion about whether or not you should face your good direction or have your back to it. When you are alone and really need to concentrate, it is ideal to have your back to a good personal direction. It is like having a good support behind you. When you are communicating with others as in the previous illustration, facing your good direction can be just as effective.

When you go to sleep at night, you lie down and the top of your head points to a certain compass direction. You are plugging yourself into a cosmic line of energy that is either going to drain you or recharge you.

Since many applications are based on timing and direction, the timing of when you were born will reveal what some of your best and worst directions are. You can utilize your best directions for a number of purposes, making yourself more of a magnet for prosperity is just an edge you can give yourself.

One branch of traditional feng shui is called the Eight Mansion school and the "eight mansions" are a reference to the eight basic directions of north, south, east, west, northeast, southeast, northwest, and southwest. This same school is also referred to as the East/West School because people and directions are categorized as either easterly or westerly. The East group includes east, southeast, north, and south. The West group is west, northwest, southwest and northeast.

There are many other ways to attract wealth with feng shui solutions, and the personal wealth direction is just one way to change your relationship with your space as opposed to other remedies that may involve incorporating elements into a room. Remember, in order to know for sure what direction you are sleeping, you've got to use a compass to know the real direction your bed goes. Refer back to Chapter Two for compass reading guidelines if you need to.

How to Win Friends and Influence People

There is a secondary personal wealth direction that works in a slightly different way than the first one just described. Some people appear successful without any help from others, even in spite of others trying to sabotage their efforts. This next wealth direction for you to consider using can bring you greater career opportunities by virtue of bringing benefactors into your life. Having a support team, or just someone who can give you a break, a tip, or a helping hand can make all the difference in the world.

Attract Supportive Friends and Benefactors Chart

Female birth year	Helpful support direction	Male birth year	Helpful support direction
1970	North	1970	North
1971	South	1971	West
1972	Northwest	1972	East
1973	Northeast	1973	Southeast
1974	Southwest	1974	Northwest
1975	Northwest	1975	Southwest
1976	Southeast	1976	Northeast
1977	East	1977	West
1978	West	1978	South
1979	North	1979	North
1980	South	1980	West
1981	Northwest	1981	East
1982	Northeast	1982	Southeast
1983	Southwest	1983	Northwest
1984	Northwest	1984	Southwest
1985	Southeast	1985	Northeast
1986	East	1986	West
1987	West	1987	South

You can use your "benefactors" direction in the exact same way as your personal wealth direction: for sleeping, choosing the best entry door, positioning a desk, and so forth.

Family Harmony and a Good Public Image

This direction can be utilized by you to help generate good will both inside and outside the home. It can also help nurture personal family harmony. Sometimes this is a lot more important than the wealth directions just described. If you have a job where you represent a public figure or you are professionally associated with a company striving for a positive image, then this public and private harmony direction can help you appear to others as likeable and trustworthy.

Public and Private Harmony Direction Chart

Female birth year	Public and private harmony direction	Male birth year	Public and private harmony direction
1970	Southeast	1970	Southeast
1971	East	1971	Northwest
1972	West	1972	South
1973	Southwest	1973	North
1974	Northeast	1974	West
1975	West	1975	Northeast
1976	North	1976	Southwest
1977	South	1977	Northwest
1978	Northwest	1978	East
1979	Southeast	1979	Southeast
1980	East	1980	Northwest
1981	West	1981	South
1982	Southwest	1982	North
1983	Northeast	1983	West
1984	West	1984	Northeast
1985	North	1985	Southwest
1986	South	1986	Northwest
1987	Northwest	1987	East

Again, after identifying your public and private harmony direction on the above chart, see if you can find ways to use it, as described for the personal wealth direction.

Your Personal Creativity Direction

Everyone has a creativity direction. It is based on your Chinese zodiac sign and then utilized within your home or workplace. When you can use your creativity direction, you become more productive, lucky, and sometimes famous or well-known. Below is a chart where you can identify your Chinese zodiac sign for the formulas that will follow. Just like the personal trigram system, the calendar beings on February 4 rather than January 1. (The personal trigrams repeat every nine years, but the Chinese zodiac signs repeat every twelve years.)

Chinese Zodiac Sign Chart

Rat	1948	1960	1972	1984	1996
Ox	1949	1961	1973	1985	1997
Tiger	1950	1962	1974	1986	1998
Rabbit	1951	1963	1975	1987	1999
Dragon	1952	1964	1976	1988	2000
Snake	1953	1965	1977	1989	2001
Horse	1954	1966	1978	1990	2002
Sheep	1955	1967	1979	1991	2003
Monkey	1956	1968	1980	1992	2004
Rooster	1957	1969	1981	1993	2005
Dog	1958	1970	1982	1994	2006
Pig	1959	1971	1983	1995	2007

Following is the Creativity Direction Chart. Find your personal creativity direction and then continue reading for the various ways you can activate your creativity direction.

Creativity Direction Chart

Your zodiac sign	Creativity direction	Precise degrees
Rat	North 2	352.5–7.5
Ox	North 2	352.5–7.5
Tiger	NE 3	52.5–67.5
Rabbit	East 2	82.5–97.5
Dragon	East 2	82.5–97.5
Snake	SE 3	142.5–157.5
Horse	South 2	172.5–187.5
Sheep	South 2	172.5–187.5
Monkey	SW 3	232.5–247.5
Rooster	West 2	262.5–277.5
Dog	West 2	262.5–277.5
Pig	NW 3	322.5–337.5

Important Note: It is correct in the chart that some Zodiac signs have the same creativity direction, such as South 2 for both the horse and the sheep signs.

The number listed after each direction specifies the subsection of that direction. For example, each direction has 3 subsections. "North 2" means the middle subsection of north. NW3 means the third subsection of NW, which is close to north. You may want to refer to the compass illustration in Chapter One, to get used to how these directions look around the perimeter of a compass as opposed to just looking at them on a chart.

A person born in 1961 is born in the Year of the Ox. Referring to the creativity direction chart, you will see that a person born in the Year of the Ox has North 2 or (N2) as their creativity direction. This sector of north is sometimes called the Rat direction. That's right, the Rat direction is the creativity direction for the Ox!

Sleep with your head pointing to your creativity direction.

Figure 4I illustrates a person born in the Year of the Rooster, sleeping with his head toward his creativity direction.

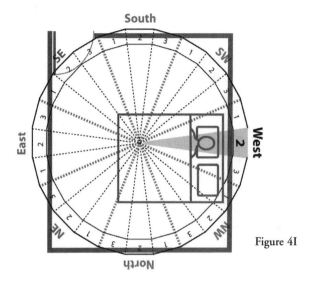

Figure 4I

Enter your home through your creativity direction. For a person born in the year of the Horse, entering through the south sector is his or her creativity direction (Figure 4J).

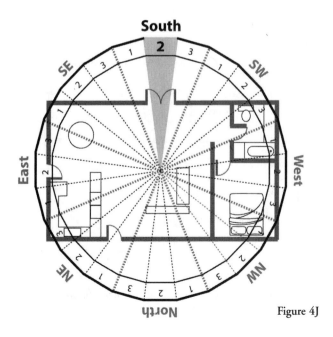

Figure 4J

Enter your workplace or an individual room through your creativity direction. For the person born in the year of the Rabbit, entering a room through the east sector will encourage his or her creativity direction (Figure 4K).

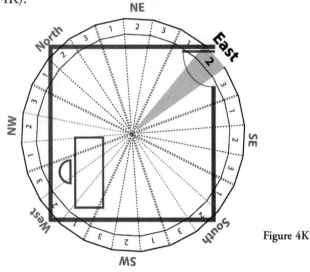

Figure 4K

Work in your creativity direction. This art studio lands in the SE3 direction, which is good for the Snake person (Figure 4L).

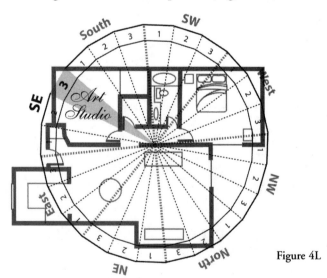

Figure 4L

Remember, your Chinese zodiac sign *is **not the same** as your personal trigram.*

In order to see whether or not you can access your creativity direction location in your current home or workplace, you need to have a floor plan sketch, an accurate compass reading of the space, and the ability to chart out (using the sector method) all the twenty-four feng shui directions.

Make a transparency copy of the compass illustration in Chapter One and place it over your floor plan sketch, according to the real compass alignment of your house. This is going to reveal exactly where your creativity direction is in your house and whether or not it lands where you can use it sensibly.

Your Personal Cosmic Savings Account

This "Lucky Money Spot" is an area where you can store your spare change and the universe will acknowledge this effort on your part. Consider the action of putting your spare change in this spot as if it were a cosmic savings account. *For every action there is a reaction.*

Your Lucky Money Spot is determined based on the last digit of the year you were born. It is related to the "Stems" in the Branch and Stem system in Four Pillars Astrology. But it should not be confused with your Chinese zodiac sign. This can perplex some people who are familiar only with the animal sign associated with their year of birth, called a "year branch."

The ten stems repeat every ten years and the 12 branches repeat every twelve years. This is why you will have two people born under the same zodiac sign, but they will not have identical energies. There are five elements that cycle through the branch system, which adds more distinctiveness to each individual's personalities. So, for example, a person could be classified as a wood Rooster, a fire Rooster, an earth Rooster, a metal Rooster, a water Rooster, and so forth for all of the Chinese zodiac signs. With twelve zodiac signs and five elements, this is why a complete cycle repeats every sixty years (12 x 5 = 60).

A person born in 1957 is a fire Rooster. A person born in 1969 is a wood Rooster. They are both Roosters, but they have their differences. This helps explain why in any given year, if it is universally known to be a good or bad year for that particular sign, still some people in that sign will do better than others.

Lucky Money Spot

With the following Lucky Money Chart, you will look at the column for the last digit of your year of birth. Then there will be a correlation to another zodiac sign, *not the year Branch you may already be familiar with*. The year Stem repeats every ten years and does not include all the zodiac signs. (You will notice on the chart below that the Dragon, Sheep, Dog, and Ox signs are missing on this list.) By the way, the Dragon, Sheep, Dog, and Ox all happen to be "earth" signs.

The direction that is associated with your year Stem will be the correct place for you to store your spare change. That's it. You just need to make a regular deposit of spare change to that location. Keep in mind that if you were born between January 1 and February 3, you are a year older. For example, a person born on February 1, 1962, would not look at the chart for birth years ending in the number 2. Instead, they would be a part of the 1961 cycle and therefore refer to the chart for years ending in 1.

Lucky Money Chart

Year of Birth	Animal Stem Direction	Location for Lucky Money Bowl	Element and Color to Use for Bowl
1940, 1950, 1960, 1970, 1980, 1990	Monkey SW3	SW3	red ceramic bowl
1941, 1951, 1961, 1971, 1981, 1991	Rooster W2	W2	yellow ceramic or metal bowl
1942, 1952, 1962, 1972, 1982, 1992	Pig NW3	NW3	yellow ceramic or metal bowl
1943, 1953, 1963, 1973, 1983, 1993	Rat N2	N2	white, silver or gold metal bowl
1944, 1954, 1964, 1974, 1984, 1994	Tiger NE3	NE3	red ceramic bowl

Year of Birth	Animal Stem Direction	Location for Lucky Money Bowl	Element and Color to Use for Bowl
1945, 1955, 1965, 1975, 1985, 1995	Rabbit E3	E3	blue or black wooden bowl
1946, 1956, 1966, 1976, 1986, 1996	Snake SE3	SE3	blue or black wooden bowl
1947, 1957, 1967, 1977, 1987, 1997	Horse S2	S2	green or red wooden bowl
1948, 1958, 1968, 1978, 1988, 1998	Snake SE3	SE3	blue or black wooden bowl
1949, 1959, 1969, 1979, 1989, 1999	Horse S2	S2	green or red wooden bowl

A person born in 1977 would refer to the above chart to see that he or she should place a green or red wood bowl exactly in the south sector of his or her house. This location would be identified easiest after having done a compass reading on the entire house and then aligning a compass transparency over the floor plan sketch, as shown in Figure 4M.

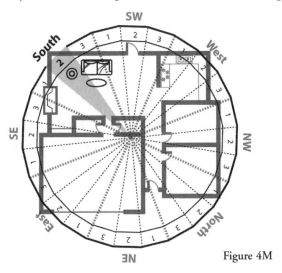

Figure 4M

The most important part of this Lucky Money Spot remedy is to put your spare change in the correction location. Secondary is the color of the bowl or the material it is made out of, to further enhance the direction. Most of my clients have noticed that this ritual of placing spare change in the right location can bring "found" money or help speed up the payment of money owed to you.

You might discover that your Lucky Money Spot falls in an area of your house that may not be practical. For instance, what if it falls in your bathroom shower? This happens sometimes, and not just with the Lucky Money Spot. Sometimes other directions that you want to take advantage of are just not accessible or practical. Don't be discouraged. Chances are there will be other prosperity remedies in this book you can incorporate in some way.

Flying Star 8

Everyone has a certain magnetic ability to attract prosperity. It happens easily when you are functioning in an area that is also drawing in prosperity. Like going from dial-up to DSL, you can speed up your prosperity potential by activating the annual 8 Star. The 8 Star is the Ken earth trigram and it is activated further with fire. Fire-colored objects and real heat produced with accent lights can be very effective.

Annual 8 Star Prosperity Chart

Northwest	North	Northeast
2011, 2020, 2029	2006, 2015, 2024	2013, 2022, 2031
West	**Center**	**East**
2012, 2021, 2030	2010, 2019, 2028	2008, 2017, 2026
Southwest	**South**	**Southeast**
2007, 2016, 2025	2005, 2014, 2023	2009, 2018, 2027

As an example, let's say your home office is in the north quadrant of your house. In 2006 and in 2015, it's like having a great enhancer to your personal luck, sitting right there with you in your office. You can further activate it with bold red color in the room and/or an accent light.

CHAPTER FIVE

I Spend;
Therefore, I Am

After reading the previous chapter on various ways you can increase your income, power, trustworthiness, and creativity, it seems imperative to also forewarn you about the ways in which your prosperity could be challenged or undermined. I have a colleague who specifically told me she conducts her consultation in phases. She first determines how to make sure her clients will stop losing money and only after they follow through with those recommendations will she deliver the information on how they can make more money. This may be something like the parental/child negotiation of, "If you eat your vegetables, you will get dessert."

I did appreciate the "incentive" approach and I empathized with her motherly perspective. It is also common that clients will often *not* do the most important remedies in the order that the consultant wishes they would so her approach is certainly organized. Still, I like to give my clients advice for both saving money and making money at exactly the same time, especially since not every remedy or theoretical correction is practical, affordable, or usable in every instance.

I discussed this with Master Sang once and enjoyed his analogy. He said, "If a person has a rotten tooth and is in a lot of pain, the dentist should pull the tooth out first, relieve the patient, and then sit down with him and instruct him on how to better take care of his other teeth." I understood this to mean that when someone is in really bad shape, try to help them get out of pain (physical, mental, financial, or spiritual) as quickly as possible, using all methods available and without holding back anything.

I cannot and should not sit in judgment of what I think someone is capable of or willing to do. In fact, I have often been pleasantly surprised by clients who exceeded my expectations in their follow through as well as the results they got.

The Draining Direction

Nearly opposite in concept to the creativity direction, the "draining direction" will make you more tired, and make it harder to save money. I have seen it with clients, as well as with myself, living in a house that is inherently good for career success and yet there are always expenditures or the inability to save the money that has been made. The draining direction often explains this discrepancy.

Some people have the draining direction "stigma" in their own personal astrology chart, regardless of where they live and saving money will always be a struggle. In other words, we can't always blame it on the house. Others may only have the draining direction problem in a certain house type or with a specific orientation of their furniture. If a person enters his or her house through his or her draining direction, even if that house has supportive feng shui for money-making, it will be challenging for that particular person to save what he or she makes.

Another way in which people activate their draining direction is if they sleep with their head pointing to that direction when they lay down at night. This direction is based on your Chinese zodiac sign and it refers to a precise magnetic compass direction within a 15-degree range.

You can look up your Chinese zodiac sign from previous charts if you do not know it by heart already. Following is the draining direction chart for each of the Chinese zodiac signs. For readers who are familiar with the directions associated with each zodiac sign, you will note that the draining direction is the exact opposite direction normally associated with the animal sign.

Draining Direction Chart

Your Zodiac Sign	Draining Direction	Precise Degrees
Rat	S2	172.5–187.5
Ox	SW1	202.5–217.5
Tiger	SW3	232.5–247.5
Rabbit	W2	262.5–277.5
Dragon	NW1	292.5–307.5
Snake	NW3	322.5–337.5
Horse	N2	352.5–7.5
Sheep	NE1	22.5–37.5
Monkey	NE3	52.5–67.5
Rooster	E2	82.5–97.5
Dog	SE1	112.5–127.5
Pig	SE3	142.5–157.5

The only remedy for the draining direction is to avoid it if possible. Avoid entering your house from that angle or sleeping with the top of your head pointing in that direction. These are cosmic lines of energy that can affect you from mildly or significantly.

In Figure 5A, a person born in the year of the Rat would be sleeping in his or her draining direction if his or her head were pointing south while sleeping.

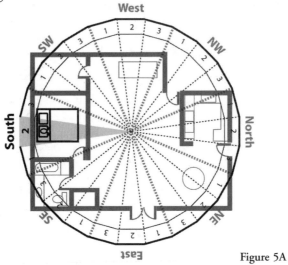

Figure 5A

Figure 5B shows a Rooster person entering his house through the east sector, which is his draining direction.

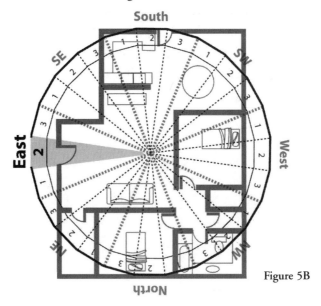

Figure 5B

Other Ways People Lose Their Money

Aside from the draining direction just described, there is another bad or unproductive sleeping direction in which someone could be positioning him- or herself. This direction is based on your personal trigram. In the chart below you will see a column that shows your year of birth and gender and an adjacent column that lists a bad direction for you to sleep in because it can make you lethargic, procrastinate, or draw financial struggles to you.

Personal Setbacks and Poor Finances Chart

Male birth year	Poor finances direction	Female birth year	Poor finances direction
1950, 1959, 1968, 1977	For K'un: north	1950, 1959, 1968, 1977	For K'an: southwest
1951, 1960, 1969, 1978	For Sun: northeast	1951, 1960, 1969, 1978	For K'un: north
1952, 1961, 1970, 1979	For Chen: west	1952, 1961, 1970, 1979	For Chen: west
1953, 1962, 1971, 1980	For K'un: north	1953, 1962, 1971, 1980	For Sun: northeast
1954, 1963, 1972, 1981	For K'an: southwest	1954, 1963, 1972, 1981	For Ken: southeast
1955, 1964, 1973, 1982	For Li: northwest	1955, 1964, 1973, 1982	For Chien: south
1956, 1965, 1974, 1983	For Ken: southeast	1956, 1965, 1974, 1983	For Tui: east
1957, 1966, 1975, 1984	For Tui: east	1957, 1966, 1975, 1984	For Ken: southeast
1958, 1967, 1976, 1985	For Chien: south	1958, 1967, 1976, 1985	For Li: northwest

These personal trigrams repeat every nine years, so if you were born before 1950, just cycle back in nine year increments from one of the years listed on the chart. If you were born after 1985, cycle forward in nine-year increments from one of the years listed on the chart to find your personal trigram and the poor finances direction associated with it.

Figure 5C shows a Li trigram person sleeping with his head to northwest, which is his draining direction.

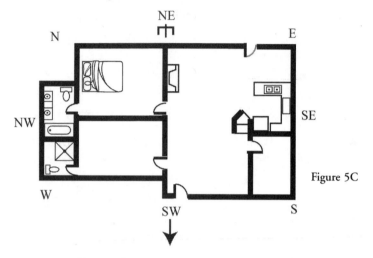

Figure 5C

As you continually reinforce your understanding of Five-Element Theory, this chart will make a lot of sense to you because the poor finances direction (the element it represents) either has a dominating effect on the personal trigram of the person, or the person's trigram has a dominating effect on the direction.

As an example, for the Li trigram person, the poor finances direction is northwest. Li is inherently fire by nature and fire destroys metal, which is the inherent element associated with northwest.

Another example: The Chien trigram people are metal in nature, and their poor finances direction is south, inherently associated with fire. Again, fire destroys metal. Either way you look at these combinations, a person will either waste a lot of their personal energy dominating that direction or they will BE dominated by the element of that direction.

Entrances

Not only is sleeping in this direction undermining, but to enter your house through this direction is also to be avoided whenever possible.

Figure 5D shows K'an trigram person entering through the southwest quadrant, his poor finances direction.

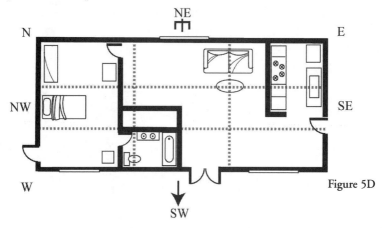

Figure 5D

Completely separate from your own personal energy, there are some entrances which are not going to be good for storing wealth, no matter who lives there. A congestive entrance is like a clogged artery. If your entrance is small and congestive, it just won't allow for enough ch'i (air currents) to enter.

Figure 5E shows an example of a congestive entrance, filled with clutter. A small entrance is like a mouth that is so small that it is difficult to get a sufficient amount of food. And the only remedy for clutter is to get rid of it.

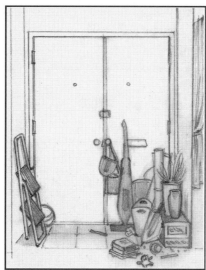

Figure 5E

Just outside the door, if there is a severe overgrowth of bushes, literally blocking light and obstructing passage, this will also choke off the good ch'i that might otherwise be able to enter the house. "Ch'i" in this regard can equal prosperity.

Don't have massive things blocking your entrance through your front door (Figure 5F).

The only remedy for an overgrown landscape is to trim it back. This might seem obvious, but some people actually think that there are mysterious cures that can be applied,

Figure 5F

like hanging chimes or bamboo flutes. Take the common sense approach instead. Similarly, if you live near an airport, hanging a crystal outside will not reduce the noise; sound-proofing and double-paned windows will reduce the noise you hear inside.

Front Door Alignments

The infamous front-door-to-back-door alignment has been written about in virtually every feng shui book. The ch'i makes a straight line from entrance to exit and the end result over time is that the occupants cannot save their money.

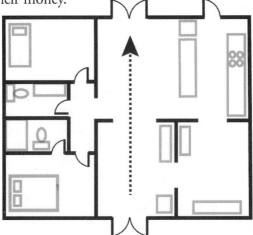

Figure 5G

Figure 5G shows the common flaw of having the front-door-to-back-door alignment. If you can avoid this kind of design layout, that is ideal. Otherwise, if you have a front door aligned directly with a back door, put live plants in between these two points. Partition screens and strategic placement of furniture can also slow down this direct path.

Figure 5H shows both a plant and a partition screen placed in between the direct alignment of two doors. Figure 5J shows a a couch positioned between the direct path of an entrance and exit door.

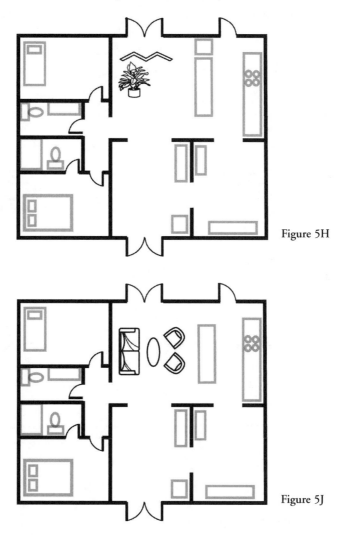

Figure 5H

Figure 5J

Staircases

A staircase that is aligned directly with a heavily used door will also create a situation where the ch'i exits the house too quickly. Translation: When the air currents escape too quickly, the money leaves too quickly.

Figure 5K shows an example of a staircase aligned directly with a front door. When you do have this predicament, placing a live plant or a water feature near the stairs can help slow down the path of ch'i. It would be ideal to also know whether or not this section of someone's house could benefit from the wood element or the water element for other reasons as well.

 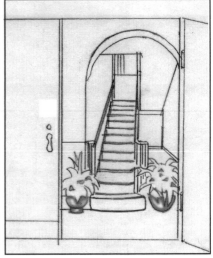

Figure 5K   Figure 5L

With this staircase aligned directly with a main door, the plant can act as a buffer to slow down the ch'i (Figure 5L).

Boundaries

Most of my local clients in Southern California live relatively close to their neighbors, yet separated from each other with fences, hedges, or high walls. Some people do not know their neighbors' names and hardly ever see them. In this regard, sometimes we can create too much of a fortress around ourselves. At least a few times per year I am asked by clients if there is any remedy for an obnoxious, noisy, or litigious neighbor.

Quite a few of my long distance clients live in areas where neighbors share the space between them, and there are no physical walls dividing the properties. At the risk of appearing un-neighborly, I have suggested they create at least a low wall to define their property and to help "shore up" and store the ch'i that enters the property on the front side so that the ch'i will not spill away in the back or on the sides. Think of ch'i as an invisible gas or liquid that needs to be contained or restrained by physical barriers.

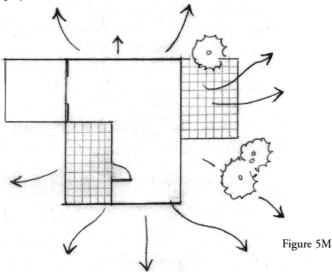

Figure 5M

Figure 5M shows a house without a surrounding fence or wall. The ch'i will get dispersed on all sides of property. Completing the surrounding walls will help the property to store the ch'i (Figure 5N).

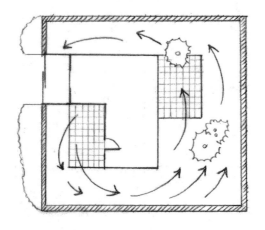

Figure 5N

Shortly after I bought my current home, I invited Master Sang and the American Feng Shui Institute over to have a case study society meeting. Although I had a fence surrounding almost my entire property, there was one opening of about 6 feet along the side of my house. The gap was from the end of the wood fence to the beginning of a thick hedge, which continued down to the street. I knew that I needed to close up this hole, but ironically I was spending so much money on other home improvements, I figured I would get to it later, maybe a few months down the road.

Master Sang made a big to-do about it, and said it was really the only uncorrected flaw he could detect. I had my contractor close up the gap with a matching fence a few days later. Coincidentally, after that fence was installed, my seemingly endless new homeowner expenditures came to a halt. Let's just say that often remedies will pay for themselves!

Figure 50 shows a house with a fence around the perimeter, but a gap in part of the fence, showing how the ch'i can leak through this area.

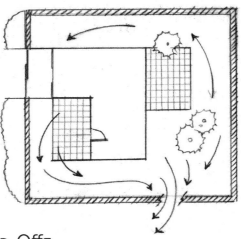

Figure 50

Land Drop Offs

Some homes, particularly those built in hilly areas, take advantage of expansive views from the backyard. No builder in his right mind would want to obstruct those views and undermine one of the selling features of the property. And yet, time and time again owners of these types of homes, with no solid back wall, and severe drop offs behind their house, will report that saving money is a struggle. Once they compromise their view a little bit with at least a two foot high wall or hedge, they report that saving gets easier.

Figure 5P

This house in Figure 5P is near the edge of a severe dropoff, with no wall or landscape to shore up the ch'i.

Alternatives to solid walls are the clear glass or acrylic material now used. It is a win/win situation because they do their job in holding the ch'i on the property, but they do not inhibit the views. These acrylic half-walls can also buffer the winds that can be typical in hilly areas or beach cities.

Top of Hill

Homes at the very top of a hill often command a huge selling price. But if there is no flat pad surrounding the home (in scale with the size of the house), and no trees or walls to create a "backing" or support, this house might also be a money pit for whoever lives there.

Figure 5Q shows a house on the very top of hill with not enough flat land surrounding it and no trees or walls for backing.

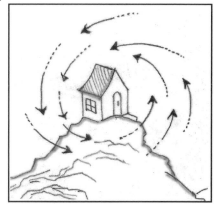

Figure 5Q

Below Street Level

One of the reasons feng shui consultants steer their clients toward the middle range on the mountain is because the very top of the hill can create problems as can the very bottom of the hill. And when a house is below street level, it cannot properly absorb or store the good ch'i, which is carried by the streets.

Figure 5R shows a house below street level, making it more difficult for the house to collect good ch'i.

Figure 5R

Traffic

When a house is level with a street, the traffic will also influence whether or not the house can properly collect the ch'i that brings prosperity. Traffic that whips by a house in high concentration and in high speeds will not be conducive to collecting the prosperity. It is no coincidence that you will rarely see large, luxurious homes on a major boulevard very close to a busy street. Usually you see only modest-sized homes

Figure 5S

and apartment buildings. Aside from the noise and pollution created by a lot of traffic, this "sha" ch'i will also accelerate the dilapidation of a building.

The house in Figure 5S is on a busy street and can be affected negatively by so many cars rushing by.

In some Asian communities you will see door frames that have been angled so that they are not parallel to the street or sidewalk. This is based on a notion that if you angle the door, it will be better able to funnel the ch'i into the building. This angling of the door can in fact redirect the "traffic" or the ch'i-flow, but there is disagreement amongst feng shui masters about just how effective this structural trick can be.

Figure 5T shows an example of the angled door aligned with street.

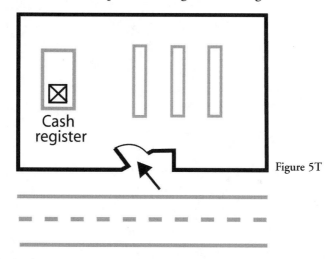

Figure 5T

Some feng shui practitioners believe this to be a highly effective measure, while others think of the angled door as an overly simplified method that reveals the lack of knowledge of more sophisticated solutions. Sometimes feng shui professionals are asked to perform miracles on buildings that are so flawed, it would have been far better to have consulted with an expert before building or buying it.

Veering Streets

In the following illustration, you see a house where the street wraps around the property and the next illustration, the street veers away from the house. Since streets carry ch'i and are considered virtual streams, the street that wraps around the property is considered more conducive to gathering wealth, while the street that approaches the house and then veers away from it is seen as causing missed opportunities.

Figure 5U shows a house where the street wraps around it. Figure 5V shows a street that veers away from a house.

Figure 5U

Figure 5V

Circular Driveways

Because of the principle just described, with streets veering away from a house as being a draining circumstance, many people assume then that a circular driveway is a miniature version of this and therefore bad as well. This is actually not the case for two reasons. The circular driveway is not really a street at all. It is so small and so few cars pass on it (usually just the owners circle around on it), that it cannot carry enough good energy away from the house to make any difference.

The half-circular driveway can also create a subtle full circle in front of a house, which is referred to as a "Ming Tang." This means "bright hall" and it is considered very lucky to have a circular arrangement in front of the house.

Figure 5X shows a circular driveway that creates an invisible circle in front of the house.

Figure 5X

Flying Stars

Finally, on a more advanced level beyond the scope of this book, there will by Flying Star configurations that can predict if an occupant will have a hard time making money or saving money based on the house type they are living in. In *Feng Shui for Skeptics*, I gave examples of some common house types based on the year of their construction that could be "bad for money" houses. This is the case regardless of street alignment or other exterior influences described in this chapter.

In Chapters One through Five, I have shared with you how different directions can affect you based on your year of birth. Some of those formulas come from Chinese astrology and some come from the East/West School. So far, from the East/West School you have learned about five of the eight basic directions in relation to your personal trigram.

The five you have learned about so far include:

1. Your best meditation direction (also good for sleeping direction)
2. The personal wealth direction
3. How to attract benefactors direction (secondary prosperity direction)
4. Public and private harmony direction
5. The personal setbacks and poor finances direction

In the next chapter, you will learn about another direction that can attract or encourage arguments and legal problems, which you will want to avoid when you can.

There are two more remaining directions, neither of which fall neatly into Chapter Four, a chapter that focuses on wealth and career. Nor do these two remaining directions exclusively relate to relationships, which is the bulk of Chapter Six. In fact, these two directions that I want to highlight for you now are very similar in their potential effect and they can undermine a person financially, physically, or emotionally. Both of these directions can cause accidents, mishaps, and illness. These unfortunate situations could affect either your personal or professional life.

Because these two negative directions are so similar, I am going to put them both in the same chart. They have distinct Chinese names, but that is not meaningful for most people reading this book and those that are already familiar with the East/West School will recognize them anyway.

The following chart shows the directions you would want to avoid sleeping in or using as an entrance, unless there were other redeeming features to those locations based on more advanced analysis.

Accidents, Mishaps, Illness Directions

Male Birth Year	Bad Directions	Female Birth Year	Bad Directions
1940, 1949, 1958	north and east	1940, 1949, 1958	west and SW
1941, 1950, 1959	south and SE	1941, 1950, 1959	NW and NE
1942, 1951, 1960	west and SW	1942, 1951, 1960	south and SE
1943, 1952, 1961	NE and NW	1943, 1952, 1961	NE and NW
1944, 1953, 1962	south and SE	1944, 1953, 1962	west and SW
1945, 1954, 1963	NW and NE	1945, 1954, 1963	east and north
1946, 1955, 1964	west and SW	1946, 1955, 1964	north and east
1947, 1956, 1965	east and north	1947, 1956, 1965	south and SE
1948, 1957, 1966	south and SE	1948, 1957, 1966	east and north

CHAPTER SIX

What's Love Got to Do With It?

Close Encounters of the Romantic Kind

There is a term in feng shui called a "peach blossom." What is a peach blossom? It is literally a flower, but the peach blossom remedy is also a symbolic reference to the delicacy of the flower being like a woman who has had her heart swept away in romance (and even heartbreak), much like the delicate peach blossom flower when it falls off the tree and gets whisked down the river.

When a man is having a "peach blossom problem" it means that he is having an affair or the complications of having an affair.

The peach blossom remedy has been written about in various forms and with various details and embellishments. The purpose of it is to help a single woman increase her ability to attract a man. We euphemistically call it "romance," although it is really indiscriminate sexual energy.

Will this remedy work for a man? To a lesser extent, yes. There are other circumstances that make it easy for a man to attract a woman; this one can sometimes work too. The romance remedy can also work well for a gay man wanting to attract another man.

I have seen the application of the peach blossom remedy result in various ways. Sometimes it just stirs up a little energy, and the woman will notice that men are paying more attention to her and/or flirting. Sometimes old boyfriends and ex-husbands start calling or showing up at the door. Sometimes totally inappropriate people seem to be attracted to the woman using the peach blossom remedy, so a conscientious consultant will always forewarn the client that she needs to be the judge of a man's character. The peach blossom remedy can increase quantity, but not guarantee quality.

After making that disclaimer, I can also say that numerous clients love the effect of the peach blossom remedy. Many get into serious, long-term relationships by using this remedy.

The Peach Blossom Romance Remedy

Based on your Chinese zodiac sign, there is a certain direction in your house that can be activated with a vase of water and fresh flowers for the purpose of attracting more romantic opportunities. There are several steps involved in applying this remedy.

First, you need to look at the chart to find out what your Chinese zodiac sign is. For people born between January 1 through February 3, remember that you are one year older when referring to the chart. For instance, a person born on January 14, 1970, would actually consider themselves born in 1969.

After you have looked up your zodiac sign, you will see that there is a direction associated with that sign. This is the location in your home where you need to place a vase of water, with flowers optional. In order to accurately know where this location is within your house, you need to use a compass and also make an accurate sketch of your floor plan. (Refer back to Chapter Two if necessary.) Don't assume your house faces a certain direction without using a compass to verify it. The compass reading must be very precise, and the remedy will not work unless you place your vase of water in the exact right location.

The water should be changed every few days if you are using just water (at least a quart in size), but change the water daily if you do have flowers in the vase. You do not want the water to become dirty or murky. The number of flowers and the color of the flowers will make the water stronger in its effect.

This feng shui remedy is for people who are trying to attract a new relationship. It is *not* for those who are already in a committed relationship. Once you are in a committed relationship, you should stop using the Romance Remedy because it may only attract people and become a distraction.

Peach Blossom Direction Chart

Rat, Dragon, or Monkey	Ox, Snake, or Rooster
1948, 1952, 1956, 1960, 1964, 1968, 1972, 1976, 1980, 1984, 1988	1949, 1953, 1957, 1961, 1965, 1969, 1973, 1977, 1981, 1984
Place a yellow or tan colored vase of water in the **W2** sector of your house. Exactly west is between 262.5-277.5 degrees.	Place a green colored vase of water in the **S2** sector of your house. Exactly south is between 172.5-187.5 degrees.
Use 2, 5 or 8 yellow or white flowers.	Use 3, 4 or 9 green, red or purple flowers.
Tiger, Horse, or Dog	**Rabbit, Sheep, or Pig**
1950, 1954, 1959, 1962, 1966, 1970, 1974, 1978, 1982, 1986	1951, 1955, 1959, 1963, 1967, 1971, 1975, 1979, 1983
Place a blue or black colored vase of water in the **E2** sector of your house. Exactly east is between 82.5–97.5 degrees.	Place a white or gold colored vase of water in the **N2** sector of your house. Exactly north is between 352.5–7.5 degrees.
Use 1, 3, or 4 blue or green flowers. An iris could be considered blue.	Use 6 or 7 white or blue flowers. A dyed blue carnation can work also.

For people born in the year of the Ox, Snake, or Rooster, they can place the vase of water in the south 2 sector of their house, as shown in Illustration 6A.

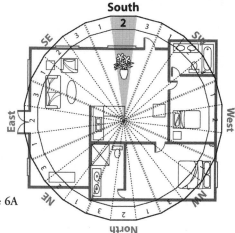

Figure 6A

The essence of this remedy is the placement of water in the right location. This is why a water fountain, unknowingly placed in someone's peach blossom remedy, can have a similar effect. When I first learned about the remedy, the only other emphasis was the color of the vase. Later I learned about using flowers and having the number and color of the flowers as further embellishments.

Clients frequently ask me about love and romance remedies when they want to attract a person to them or improve an existing relationship. The truth is that there is no guaranteed remedy or magic pill for relationships or to draw in Mr. or Ms. Right, but there are plenty of indirect ways to attract and improve relationships.

For instance, a couple who has been married for a long time will want to know if there is a way to spice up their sex life. If you believe in the propagandists of "trash feng shui," they might instruct a woman to wear sexy lingerie or keep a copy of the Kama Sutra by the bedside. As I mentioned in my first book, these are not traditional remedies, rather they are placebos. But if you look to the reasons *why* a couple may be lacking in their sex life, it could be caused by any number of stresses. To reduce the argumentative energies in a house, by definition, will help engender a cozy and calm atmosphere, more conducive to love. This is what I mean by indirect ways.

If you eliminate energies in a house that can make a person feel alienated or detached, then by definition you are going to feel more like relating sexually to your spouse. Even improving the financial status for the household can have an indirect effect on your sex life. Many men have their sexual libido very much tied to their self-esteem as it relates to their success in their careers.

Capitalizing on the Sexualized "4 Star" Energy

Similar to the peach blossom romance remedy, stimulating the Flying Star 4 in your house needs to be used with discretion and it is for single people only. In other words, stimulating it does not make an existing relationship better. In fact, some feng shui practitioners believe that when Flying Star 4 is not in a good phase, that it can create more heartache and scandal than it can attract true romance.

All of these "numbers," which represent energies that float around your house, go through good phases and bad phases. They have a complete life span of 180 years and then it repeats. The last time the 4 Star had only positive connotations was during the last Period 4 Construction Cycle of 1924–1943. Some believe the 4 Star will not start to regain its positive connotations until the year 2064. (This is the beginning of Period 2 and that is when the 4 Star will turn a corner and be positive for the ensuing sixty years.)

I still think that the 4 Star can be used, with caution, to kickstart someone's romantic opportunities. I have seen it work so many times I still include it in my list of remedies for romance.

As described in *Feng Shui for Skeptics,* there are house types that can be characterized as being very conducive to attracting love, just by having been built in the Period 4 cycle. And every house will have the 4 Star located in a couple of locations in virtually every floor plan.

What we will look at in this chapter is just the annual 4 Star. This is one of the easiest methods for feng shui beginners who do not already know the more advanced formulas to determine the permanent energies of a house. At least you can track the annual 4 Star, put a fountain in that location of your house for the current year, and let it help you attract romance.

Once again, the prerequisite steps for being able to locate the annual 4 Star in your home are:

1. Draw out a to-scale floor plan sketch.

2. Take an accurate compass reading so you know what direction your house or apartment faces.

3. Divide up your floor plan into equal divisions, and length and width into thirds to identify the directional quadrants.

The chart below will show you where the annual 4 Star will be in certain years. The 4 Star, like all the other Flying Stars, will follow a predictable pattern and then repeat that directional flow every nine years.

Annual 4 Star Chart

Northwest	North	Northeast
2006, 2015, 2024, 2033	2010, 2019, 2028, 2037	2008, 2017, 2026, 2035
West	**Center**	**East**
2007, 2016, 2025, 2034	2005, 2014, 2023, 2032	2012, 2021, 2030, 2039
Southwest	**South**	**Southeast**
2011, 2020, 2029, 2038	2009, 2018, 2027, 2036	2013, 2022, 2031, 2040

After locating where the annual 4 Star is in your house in any given year, place a water fountain in that area and run the fountain as much as possible. If the fountain ends up being placed in a wakeful room (living room, dining room, kitchen) then you can keep the fountain on all the time.

If the fountain needs to be in your bedroom for the year, then it is up to you if you want to run it all the time or just turn it off at night when you are in the room sleeping. Some people are relaxed by the background sounds of water trickling in their bedroom and for others it becomes a disturbance. A very famous feng shui personality has promoted the notion that you should never have a fountain in your bedroom. This is absolutely not true. Sometimes it is the most important remedy a person can place in their home.

Feng shui tip: If your fountain needs to be in the bedroom, plug it into an electronic timer so that you don't have to think about turning it on and off every day.

Happiness and Fertility

In the same way that you can track and stimulate the yearly 4 Star for increased romance, the Flying Star 8 is associated with bringing happiness and happy events like weddings. But it is also associated with fertility, so be careful if you do not want to get pregnant.

When the annual Flying Star 8 comes to your front door or your bedroom, it indicates a year when you are more likely to have a happy event in the making. The Flying Star 8 is also associated with prosperity, so to activate it can definitely be considered a wealth remedy as previously described in Chapter Four.

Below is a chart that tracks the Flying Star 8 on an annual basis, so you can see where it will be each year for many years to come.

Annual 8 Star Chart

Northwest	North	Northeast
2011, 2020, 2029, 2038	2006, 2015, 2024, 2033	2013, 2022, 2031, 2040
West	**Center**	**East**
2012, 2021, 2030, 2039	2010, 2019, 2028, 2037	2008, 2017, 2026, 2035
Southwest	**South**	**Southeast**
2007, 2016, 2025, 2034	2014, 2023, 2032, 2041	2009, 2018, 2027, 2036

This 8 Star is the Ken trigram, inherently earth in its nature. The way to stimulate earth is with fire. This means placing a largely red-colored item in the room when the annual 8 Star resides in that location. You could also use a high-intensity light or an accent light to create the fire element in a room.

This can stimulate getting pregnant, getting married, or receiving more income. If you only want one of these things, such as more income but not getting pregnant, then you are well advised to get professional assistance to deepen your feng shui analysis. You do not want to inadvertently get one outcome when you wanted something else instead. I guess this might be the feng shui interpretation of "playing with fire." Pun intended!

Energies That Can Make You Lonely or Depressed

In this chapter about relationships, it is important to try to cancel out influences that might otherwise sabotage a perfectly good relationship or prevent a new one from beginning. Tracking and curing the annual 2 Star is one effective method.

In the following chart you will see the familiar directional quadrants and the grouping of years when the annual 2 Star will be residing in these directions. I have found this annual 2 to be quite predictable in determining when a person may have separated from his or her spouse, broken off an engagement, or simply ended a relationship. Armed with this knowledge, you can address the annual 2 in your house by weakening it with metal.

Remember, metal is anything made out of copper, brass, bronze, iron, steel, and various other metallic substances, even aluminum. For an average-sized room, have at least 50 to 80 pounds of metal. For a larger room, add more. You can hardly overdo the metal, although with more advanced understanding of the space (based on when it was built) you might be conservative with the metal for other reasons.

Many schools recommend that "moving" metal be used to cure the negative earth Stars. I recommend metal pendulum clocks and chimes as well, but obviously not for a bedroom that might need metal. Save your moving metal remedies for "yang" areas, such as entrances and offices.

There are other benefits to adding metal in a room where there is an annual 2 Star. The annual 2 can draw in sickness, bleeding, miscarriage, or abdominal problems, so the metal can help with health issues as much as relationship problems.

The Annual 2 Star Chart

Northwest	North	Northeast
2008, 2017,	2012, 2021,	2010, 2019,
2026, 2035	2030, 2039	2028, 2037
West	**Center**	**East**
2009, 2018,	2007, 2016,	2014, 2023,
2027, 2036	2025, 2034	2032, 2041
Southwest	**South**	**Southeast**
2013, 2022,	2011, 2020,	2006, 2015,
2031, 2040	2029, 2038	2024, 2033

The annual 2 Star happens to be the earth element, which is why adding metal will weaken it. The annual 8 Star is earth as well, but in the previous section, it was advised to enhance it with fire. In the scope of feng shui remedies, this is a common goal: to enhance the positives and to reduce the negatives.

As powerful as these corrections can be, it is also important not to have the wrong elements present. This could trigger the annuals negatively and defeat the point of adding the corrective cure.

Here is another way of looking at it:

● An annual 2 Star in a bedroom could cause health or relationship problems.

● An annual 2 Star in a bedroom with red color will almost *certainly cause problems.*

● An annual 2 Star in a bedroom with sufficient metal can *prevent such problems.*

Having just described the K'un trigram as the annual 2 Star, it should be understood that if the K'un Trigram is your *personal trigram*, it absolutely does not mean that you are prone to being depressed, lonely, or sickly. The annual stars take on distinct meanings that are *not* a reflection of the people who share that trigram as their own. In addition, following is a description of the 3 Star. People who are the Chen *personal trigram* should not construe the annual meaning to be a reflection of who they are either.

Energies That Can Make You More Argumentative

In order to increase the chances of having better communication with loved ones, it is practical to subdue the very forces that can kick up arguments, bickering, or gossip.

The annual 3 Star roams around from direction to direction just like all the other annual influences. The 3 Star is the Chen trigram, described as "hard wood" for the element it represents. In Five-Element Theory, wood is consumed by fire. It is weakened that way. So by adding fire to the location of the annual 3, you can reduce potential arguments, bickering, or gossip. This does surprise people, that a stimulating color like red, could actually *calm down* energies, but it does.

Below is a chart that tracks for you the location of the annual 3 Star for many years to come. Keep in mind that this annual influence, like other annual influences, will not affect you much unless it lands in an area of your home where you spend at least an hour per day.

Annual 3 Star Chart

Northwest	North	Northeast
2007, 2016	2011, 2020	2009, 2018
West	**Center**	**East**
2008, 2017	2006, 2015	2013, 2022
Southwest	**South**	**Southeast**
2012, 2021	2010, 2019	2005, 2014

Keeping track of this 3 Star is like being ahead of the game and able to plan accordingly. Since so many of my clients have been able to control this energy after they learn about it, there is no question you can remedy these areas just before their yearly influence starts and possibly avoid their negative impact altogether.

Tracking the annual 5 Star can be just as effective as remedying the annual 3 Star when trying to create more harmony and better communication in your life. All the numbers/stars have a multitude of meanings, especially when they are combined in more advanced readings, such as the permanent stars created based on when the entire structure is built. But it is in the *annual cycles* that things happen on cue and the 5 Star's presence can cause arguments, pain, or accidents. More so than the 3 Star, this 5 Star influence could contribute to physical harm as much as the emotional toll it can have on people.

I do have clients who seem to coexist with a permanent 5 Star in their house, with metal remedies in place, and they do not have any extraordinary problems. But at the same time, when someone is doing badly, an unremedied 5 Star is almost always playing some kind of role in that location (as a permanent star, annual star, or monthly star).

Below is a chart that tracks the annual 5 Star for many years to come. The same directional progression of the annual star exists for each one, in the same pattern of center, northwest, west, northeast, south, north, southwest, east, and southeast, then starting the cycle over again. The 5 Star is earth in nature, so generous amounts of metal objects will weaken it or cancel it out completely.

Annual 5 Star Chart

Northwest	North	Northeast
2005, 2014	2009, 2018	2007, 2016
West	**Center**	**East**
2006, 2015	2013, 2022	2011, 2020
Southwest	**South**	**Southeast**
2010, 2019	2008, 2017	2012, 2021

Going back to the East/West School, everyone has a certain direction based on their year of birth that can make them more argumentative if the person spends a lot of time in that direction. There is no remedy for it like the Flying Stars, which respond to real elements. Instead, the direction that is bad for you personally, and that can potentially make you argumentative, should just be *avoided* whenever possible. This is like avoiding another individual who brings out the worst in you, where the best course of action is to not let yourself even get into a confrontational situation to begin with.

Below is a chart that tells you what direction to avoid if you want to escape the potential for flare ups. This direction is based on your personal trigram. Does this mean you cannot ever use this direction or pass through it? No, it just means this is a direction to avoid holding an important meeting or conversation in when emotions could get agitated. It is not a good direction for you, so you want to avoid using it as an entrance or as a sleeping direction if at all possible.

Your Personal "Prone to Argue" Direction (to Avoid)

For *Males*	For *Females*
1952,1961, 1970, 1979 southwest	1952, 1961, 1970, 1979 southwest
1953, 1962., 1971,1980 east	1953, 1962, 1971, 1980 northwest
1972, 1981, 1990, 1999 west	1972, 1981, 1990, 1999 south
1973,1982, 1991, 2000 northeast	1973, 1982, 1991, 2000 southeast
1974, 1983, 1992, 2001 south	1974, 1983, 1992, 2001 north
1975, 1984, 1993, 2002 north	1975, 1984, 1993, 2002 south
1976, 1985, 1994, 2003 southeast	1976, 1985, 1994, 2003 northeast
1977, 1986, 1995, 2004 east	1977, 1986, 1995, 2004 west
1978, 1987, 1996, 2005 northwest	1978, 1987, 1996, 2005 east

Portable Remedies

By now, you may have concluded that having some portable remedies are in order when it comes to the Flying Star part of feng shui. This is true! When you purchase a fountain, you might consider a style or size that could work in your bedroom as much as near your entry way or another room.

Having a fire element remedy, such as an accent light, could be moved around to the appropriate location from year to year.

Metal objects that are functional, decorative, or hidden can also be shifted to different locations, as needed.

Personal Compatibility With Others

Using the Chinese solar calendar, each person is a certain element based on the year of birth and gender. This should not be confused with the Chinese astrology system, which does not differentiate for gender. Personal trigram compatibility is based on Five-Element Theory.

- Since water nurtures wood, people who are the K'an trigram (water) will be very supportive to people who are the Chen or Sun trigrams (both are the wood element).

- People who are the Chen or Sun trigrams (wood) will nurture those born under the Li (fire) trigram.

- People born under the Li (fire) trigram will nurture the earth trigram people.

- K'un and Ken are both earth trigrams. The K'un and Ken (earth) trigram people will nurture the metal people. The metal trigrams are Tui and Chien.

- Finally, the Tui and Chien trigram people(metal trigrams) will nurture the K'an (water) trigram people.

This nurturing relationship can be found between couples, spouses, parents to children, siblings, friends, and coworkers. It helps explain who is the giver and who is the taker within a relationship. It helps explain the easy, supportive relationships.

Consistent with Five-Element Theory, people who are in a domination cycle with each other may have some power struggles or the relationships may be more controlling or draining:

- A K'an (water) person will dominate a Li (fire) person.
- A Li (fire) person will dominate a Tui or Chien (metal) person.
- A Tui or Chien (metal) person will dominate a Chen or Sun (wood) person.
- A Chen or Sun (wood) person will dominate a K'un or Ken (earth) person.
- A K'un or Ken (earth) person will dominate a K'an (water) person.

The way I have just defined these relationships is based only on the elements and whether or not the trigrams (as elements) are in a productive or domination cycle with each other. In contrast, the East/West school divides the eight trigrams into two groups and their compatibility relationship is based on that alone.

For instance, the "west" type people are Ken, K'un, Tui, and Chien. These happen to be all of the earth and metal trigrams. Even in Five-Element Theory, earth always supports metal, so there is no contradiction in saying that all of the west type people happen to be compatible because they are all matching or complementary to each other as elements.

With the "east" type people, you have Sun, Chen, Li, and K'an. There is one domination relationship within this east group. It is Li and K'an. This has been described as water dominating fire, and yet they are both east group trigrams. So, are they compatible as east group people or are they not compatible as elements? The answer is that they are compatible, but one is controlling the other. It is just a subtle difference from the other trigrams.

This is just one example of the mixed messages that do exist in feng shui theory, like one direction that might be good for a certain aspect of your life and not another.

The Opposition Signs in Chinese Astrology

As just described, there are personal trigrams that can be in conflict with each other, but there is another system that can also reveal similar power struggles or communication problems. The year of birth might be the most superficial piece of information within a comprehensive Chinese Astrology analysis. The year of birth can explain the influences of your grandparents on your own life. Then, the month of birth can reflect the influence of your parents. The day of birth can explain your relationship with your spouse and the hour of birth can symbolize the influence of your children. Still, the year of birth can deliver much information regarding your basic personality and in one aspect, what sign you may have a particular conflict with in a romantic or spousal relationship.

The word "chong" can be translated as "something rushing toward you." It also implies an opposition force. The Chinese zodiac sign that opposes you is the sign that is the exact opposite of yours. Since there are twelve Chinese zodiac signs representing each year, people who are six years older than you or six years younger than you will always be in that "chong" or opposition direction to you. This would also be true for anyone eighteen or thirty years older or younger than you.

If you find that you are beginning a relationship where the person's zodiac sign is in opposition to yours, do not automatically or impulsively end the relationship. But consider yourself put on notice that there might be conflicts. I would recommend getting a very detailed compatibility astrology reading to see if there are any redeeming or compensating aspects to the two charts. Sometimes, a couple can have a yearly opposition chart, but their month, day, and hour signs are much more harmonious.

Chong "Opposition" Chart:

Your Zodiac Sign (Repeats each 12 years)	The Zodiac Sign that Opposes You
Ox 1937, 1949, 1961, 1973, 1985, 1997	**Sheep** 1931, 1943, 1955, 1967, 1979, 1991
Tiger 1938, 1950, 1962, 1974, 1986, 1998	**Monkey** 1932, 1944, 1956, 1968, 1980
Rabbit 1939, 1951, 1963, 1975, 1987, 1999	**Rooster** 1933, 1945, 1957, 1969, 1981
Dragon 1940, 1952, 1964, 1976, 1988	**Dog** 1934, 1946, 1958, 1970, 1982, 1994
Snake 1941, 1953, 1965, 1977, 1989, 2001	**Pig** 1935, 1947, 1959, 1971, 1983, 1995
Horse 1942, 1954, 1966, 1978, 1990, 2002	**Rat** 1936, 1948, 1960, 1972, 1984, 1996
Sheep 1943, 1955, 1967, 1979, 1991, 2003	**Ox** 1937, 1949, 1961, 1973, 1985, 1997
Monkey 1944, 1956, 1968, 1980, 1992	**Tiger** 1938, 1950, 1962, 1974, 1986, 1998
Rooster 1945, 1957, 1969, 1981, 1993	**Rabbit** 1939, 1951, 1963, 1975, 1987, 1999
Dog 1946, 1958, 1970, 1982, 1994, 2006	**Dragon** 1940, 1952, 1964, 1976, 1988
Pig 1947, 1959, 1971, 1983, 1995, 2007	**Snake** 1941, 1953, 1965, 1977, 1989, 2001
Rat 1948, 1960, 1972, 1984, 1996, 2008	**Horse** 1942, 1954, 1966, 1978, 1990, 2002

Lonely Sleeping Direction

The proper alignment of furnishings can control how air currents move through a room, creating balance. Human beings can also create balance or imbalance based on how they align themselves within a room and the directions relative to that space. Your east is someone else's west. The "lonely sleeping" direction implies that if you sleep with your head pointing to a certain direction, you could be sabotaging your efforts or desire to be partnered. We have that saying of "being on the same wavelength" and the lonely sleeping direction is like placing yourself on a wavelength that is not harmonious for encouraging your connectedness to other human beings, especially that someone who may otherwise be drawn to you.

The following chart shows the 15-degree compass alignment that you would need to be sleeping in to create this negative circumstance.

Lonely Sleeping Direction Chart

Your Chinese Zodiac Sign	*Males* Lonely Sleeping Direction	*Females* Lonely Sleeping Direction
Rat	NE3	NW1
Ox	NE3	NW1
Tiger	SE3	NE1
Rabbit	SE3	NE1
Dragon	SE3	NE1
Snake	SW3	SE1
Horse	SW3	SE1
Sheep	SW3	SE1
Monkey	NW3	SW1
Rooster	NW3	SW1
Dog	NW3	SW1
Pig	NE3	NW1

The "No Marriage" House

The unique relationship between you and your house cannot be overestimated. Although there are lots of effective and powerful remedies that can improve quality of life for any person, there are some feng shui circumstances that cannot be changed. We can use a grown adult as an example. If an overweight adult wants to lose 20 pounds, it can be done.

If he wants to be 6 inches taller, it's not going to happen. The "no marriage house" needs to be avoided because there is no remedy for it.

Based on your Chinese zodiac sign, there is a certain house type that can sabotage your ability to get married. You have to be comfortable using a compass in order to determine this. The precise compass direction is a narrow 15-degree increment, so you have to be very careful doing your compass reading. The direction to be concerned with is called the "sitting" side of the house. This is basically just the back wall of the house.

The sitting side of a house is considered its real character or strength, just like the back or spine of a person. So, if the back/sitting direction is incompatible with your own zodiac sign, then it will interfere with your ability to attract a serious partner. If you moved into this house type after marrying, it could also undermine the existing relationship.

Refer to the chart below to determine your zodiac sign and the direction that your house should not be backed up to if you want more than anything to be married. Keep in mind that February 4 begins each year, not January 1, when using every birth year formula in this book. If you were born in January 1962, you would consider yourself born in 1961 instead.

No Marriage House Chart

Your zodiac sign (the sign repeats every twelve years)	Bad direction for your house to be backed up to (for the purpose of attraction)
Tiger 1950, 1962, 1974, 1986	East 2 82.5–97.5 degrees
Rabbit 1951, 1963, 1975, 1987	SE 1 112.5 –127.5 degrees
Dragon 1952, 1964, 1976, 1988	SE 3 142.5 –157.5 degrees
Snake 1953, 1965, 1977, 1989	South 2 172.5 –187.5 degrees
Horse 1954, 1966, 1978, 1990	SW 1 202.5 –217.5 degrees
Sheep 1955, 1967, 1979, 1991	SW 3 232.5 –247.5 degrees
Monkey 1956, 1968, 1980, 1992	West 2 262.5 –277.5 degrees
Rooster 1957, 1969, 1981, 1993	NW 1 292.5 –307.5 degrees
Dog 1958, 1970, 1982, 1994	NW 3 322.5 –337.5 degrees
Pig 1959, 1971, 1983, 1995	North 2 352.5 –7.5 degrees
Rat 1960, 1972, 1984, 1996	NE 1 22.5 –37.5 degrees
Ox 1949, 1961, 1973, 1985	NE 3 52.5 –67.5 degrees

How Important Is the Wedding Date?

Frequently, I can evaluate a person's home and predict the likelihood of him or her meeting someone new for a romantic encounter that year, and in some cases I can narrow it down to the most likely months. When the potential is high to meet someone new, that is not the month to go into hibernation. So I will advise a client to be available for this opportunity in time, when the house can actually help them attract someone.

Then, at least a few times per year, clients will ask whether or not I can help them choose a wedding date. This kind of advice is best left in the hands of a competent astrologer, who can look at the individual charts for each person, see how their energies combine, and then choose a date that can energetically fill in any deficiencies in the relationship. This is especially critical for couples who already have communication problems or issues which might undermine their commitment to each other.

But here's the kicker: The wedding date is often not as influential as you might hope it to be. In the past, the wedding date was in fact the time that established when a couple would truly start living together under one roof and unite their destinies. It even meant in many cases that this would be the first time the couple would have sex (a.k.a. the wedding night). Well, that is certainly rarely the case nowadays!

When a couple actually starts *living together* is the really important date. Some couples live together for years before they officially tie the knot. If you are considering living with your boyfriend or girlfriend and want to initiate this on the most positive date, have a competent Chinese astrologer calculate for you what has historically been called the Marriage Selection Date. If you are already living together and plan to officially marry, you can still use another good Marriage Selection Date. These days, relationships need all the positive reinforcement they can get.

CHAPTER SEVEN

The Hidden Agenda of Your House

The Center of Your House and What Activates It

Every house has a hidden potential. This is based on when the house was built and what direction it is sitting and facing. In Flying Star feng shui, it is revealed as a calculation with a set of numbers placed in the center of a house's floor plan that represent the unseen influences in that area and throughout the whole house.

Unlike other sections in a house, where the energies are pretty much confined to those directional areas, the center area is different. It represents energy that permeates the entire house. You can think of the energy at the center of a house like its core or navel point. This energy then radiates out to fill the entire house. Another way to look at it is with the metaphor of a person. You have an arm and a leg and a head and they are in distinct locations on your body. But your personality is a part of you that runs through every cell. It cannot be confined or pinpointed to residing in just one location.

The center of a house is often—literally—a pass-through area such as a hallway. Sometimes it includes part of a room that is actually used, but more often than not it is a transition area.

In Figure 7A you can see a floor plan where the occupant is using a corner of their bedroom to position a desk. This just happens to end up in the very center of the house. So whatever hidden potential resides in the center of this house, it will be more active and less "hidden" when the center of the house is actually used.

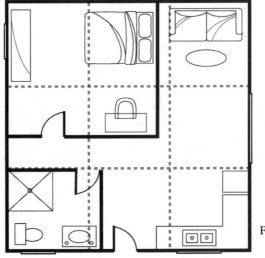

Figure 7A

More Examples of Design and Architecture That Stimulate the Center

If a house has an extension to its basic body, then this is like someone stretching out their arm or leg. If I were to pull your arm or leg, you would also feel the stretch in your chest or torso. Essentially, I would be stimulating the center of your body. In Figure 7B you can see an example of a house with an extended quadrant. Whatever is determined to be the central energy of that house, it is likely to be more active than a house without extensions.

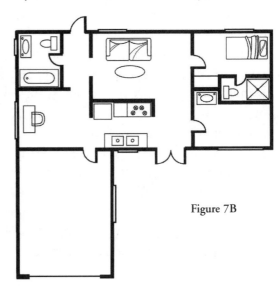

Figure 7B

In Figure 7C, there is a floor plan with no extensions to further stimulate the center of the house.

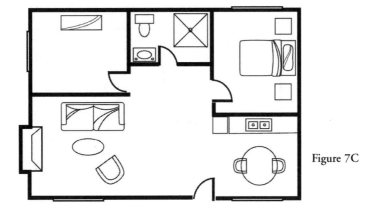

Figure 7C

Other ways the center energy of a house can be more active include the following:

- A staircase in the center of the house (see Figure 7D). This is because people are moving up and down the stairs, often quickly and the shape of the stairs can further stimulate the area.

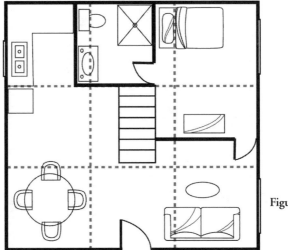

Figure 7D

- A bathroom in the center of the house (see Figure 7E). For the same reasons as the staircase, a toilet's flushing of water or the frequent use of the sink can further activate that area of the house.

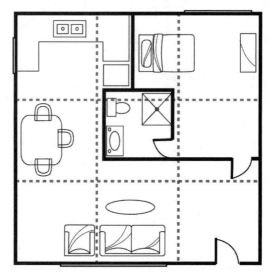

Figure 7E

- A door in the center of the house, such as a door leading to outside space or a garage (see Figures 7F and 7G).

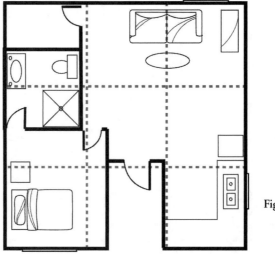

Figure 7F

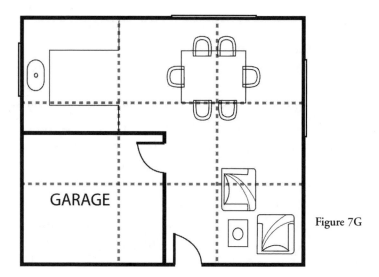

Figure 7G

- The stove brings in the fire element and when it is in the center of a house, it is usually a negative. There are exceptions, however.

As in Figure 7H, it is usually not good to have a stove or oven right in the center of the house.

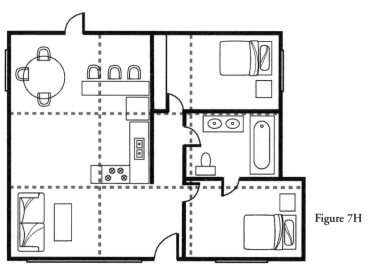

Figure 7H

What the Center of a House Indicates

With the center of the house being the "soul" of the house, the potential energy there can set the tone or influence how the occupants will do in this entire house. Frankly, most houses have a negative center. Does that mean no house has good feng shui? No, but the shape of the house, along with who is living there, can either activate or suppress what is inherently a personality trait of that structure.

What follows in this upcoming section is a run down of all the basic house types, according to the Flying Star School. The two coordinates that determine these house types are the year they are built and direction they are facing. In classical feng shui studies, houses are usually referenced according to their *sitting* direction as opposed to their facing direction.

The sitting side is emphasized a number of times, such as in determining the best color for the exteriors or what constitutes the "no marriage house." But for the layperson reading this, I have simply chosen to use the facing side of the house as the directional reference, since that is the side that most people can relate to easily without any feng shui training. For the sake of this chapter, we will assume in every case that the facing side is parallel to the sitting side of each house. If the sitting and facing sides of your house are *not* parallel, then do not look up your house type under the facing direction. Instead, take note of the *sitting* side and then consider the opposite direction to be the facing side, just for the sake of this chapter.

As an example, if a house sits north but has an angled front side that does not face south, still consider it a south-facing house just for the sake of correctly identifying your house type in this chapter.

If a house has a negative aspect to its center, this alone is not a reason to fear the house and its effects. But you will see when reviewing this section that there are some house types that are clearly not appropriate for certain types of people, certain occupations, or chronic challenges that a person might have by living in that kind of environment.

Remember, in this particular list, I am only revealing the energy in the *center* of the house, its hidden potential. This is not the most important piece of information to even be revealed about the house. Nor should this information be the only thing you use to decide whether or not you want to buy a house or continue living in the one you are already in.

But it is a telling aspect, one of many layers. Identifying your house according to when it was built and its basic compass alignment will also not require you to learn how to do the advanced Flying Star calculations. You can just gain a piece of knowledge about a house when you know the compass alignment and the year built.

Important Note: To determine the real facing direction of your house, *you must use a compass*. Magnetic compass directions are often not in sync with true north. In the United States the discrepancy can be anywhere from 0 to 18 degrees off of true north, so just looking at a map is not sufficient enough to know for sure what direction your house faces. For example, Los Angeles County is about 13 degrees off of true north.

It is the whole facing side (front façade) of the house that will face a certain direction. Don't be fooled by a door that is really on the side of the house or an entry extension that juts out, positioning the door to open in a different direction than the *facing wall* of the house. See Figures 7I and 7J for illustrations showing doors that open up to different directions than the facing side of the house.

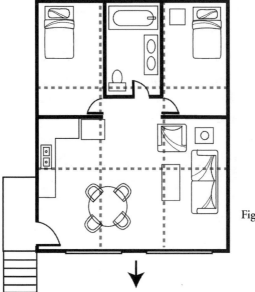

Figure 7I

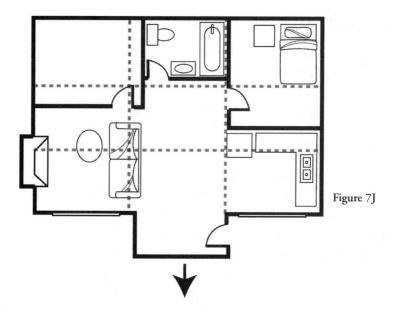

Figure 7J

Another Important Note: The interpretations given for the center of these house types is based on the current times, at the time this book was written. In other words, if a house was built a hundred years ago, it had a different effect on the occupants when it was a new house, compared to how the house affects people now. The interpretations given are only for how the house affects the people in the current Period 8 Cycle that this book was written in unless stated otherwise. Some of the house types will have a similar effect on occupants even into the Period 9 cycle (2024–2043).

Yet Another Important Note: For the benefit of readers at various levels of exposure to Flying Star feng shui, I will list the "numbers" or Flying Stars in the center of each house. Readers familiar with the Flying Stars (mountain star and water star) will be able to appreciate this quick reference to the center of each house type. Readers who are *not* familiar with the Flying Stars are not required to know how these "numbers" got to be where they are. Beginners can appreciate just the description of each house type without having to know how to do the advanced calculations.

One More Thing: Houses are built in twenty-year construction cycles. For all the house types described, the range in years should be understood as in the following example: 2004 through 2023 literally means February 4, 2004, through February 3, 2024. In other words, the last year listed for any construction cycle means all the way through the end of that year. Consequently, 1944–1963 means through the *end* of 1963. In addition to that, the month of January is always part of the annual year preceding it. February 4 begins each year. As another example, if the roof of your house went on in January 1984, then your house is part of the 1983 construction year and is a Period 6 house (1964–1983) and not part of the Period 7 Cycle (1984–2023).

In the following section, there will be quite a few houses described as being in "Money Lock" or "People Lock" phases. "Lock" should not to be confused with *luck*. The Locked phase is a time frame when a house is not going to have a good effect on the occupants. The Money Lock undermines financial success and advancements. The People Lock undermines health, relationships, and fertility.

72 Different House Types

The North-Facing House:

NORTH-FACING HOUSE, **BUILT BETWEEN 1864–1883**

- **Period 1** returns during 2044–2063
- Flying Stars in Center: 5–6
- Potential for health problems related to the upper body and head region. This house is also not good for a man over age sixty because it can undermine his health. This house could also be more problematic for people who are the Chien trigram.

NORTH-FACING HOUSE, **BUILT BETWEEN 1884–1903**

- **Period 2** returns 2064–2083
- Flying Stars in the Center: 6–7
- There is potential for occupants to argue a lot as well as for injuries, especially with metal objects. This is not a bad center for an occupant whose occupation or skills are related to self-defense, such as martial arts or police work.

NORTH-FACING HOUSE, **BUILT BETWEEN 1904–1923**

- **Period 3** returns 2084–2103
- Flying Stars in the Center: 7–8
- Good potential for the occupants to have an easy time making money, as long as they have water features in and around their house in clear view during the Period 8 Construction Cycle.

NORTH-FACING HOUSE, **BUILT BETWEEN 1924–1943**

- **Period 4** returns 2104–2123
- Flying Stars in the Center: 8–9
- Easy for occupants to be successful, but there could be any number of health problems or fertility problems unless they have inside and outside water features in clear view during the Period 8 Construction Cycle.

NORTH-FACING HOUSE, **BUILT BETWEEN 1944–1963**

- **Period 5** returns 2124–2143
- Flying Stars in the Center: 9–1
- Easy for the occupants to have heart or eye problems. A person born to the Li trigram could be especially vulnerable to heart or eye problems or injuries related to fire or explosions.

NORTH-FACING HOUSE, **BUILT BETWEEN 1964–1983**

- **Period 6** returns 2144–2163
- Flying Stars in the Center: 1–2
- Occupants could have problems with kidneys, blood, circulation, ears, or glands in general.

    People born of the K'an trigram can be especially vulnerable. This is also a house type where the woman could dominate the man, easily leading to separation since most men rebel against being dominated. I have a handful of clients who have stayed married in this kind of house, when the husband is easygoing and secure. He can let his wife take control or responsibility for many things and may even appreciate how competent she is.

NORTH-FACING HOUSE, **BUILT BETWEEN 1984–2003**

- **Period 7** returns 2164–2183
- Flying Stars in the Center: 2–3
- While this house is generally regarded as a lucky house for the good Flying Stars that often land in other important areas of the house, there is also potential for arguments, gossip, legal disputes, or health problems related to the abdominal area. People of the K'un trigram are especially vulnerable in this house type.

NORTH-FACING HOUSE, **BUILT BETWEEN 2004–2023**

- **Period 8** returns 2184–2203
- Flying Stars in the Center: 3–4
- People in this house can be very creative but also unstable emotion-

ally. Sometimes this goes hand-in-hand with the artist personality. Although other components would also have to be in place, a rare aspect to this house could also trigger an incestuous relationship between a brother and sister. What happens more frequently in this house type is the occupants could be involved with gossip and/or more common sexual indiscretions.

NORTH–FACING HOUSE BUILT, BETWEEN 1844–1863

- **Period 9** returns 2044–2063
- Flying Stars in the Center: 4–5
- People in this house can have potential problems with low back, legs, skin problems, or rheumatism. There is also potential for sexually transmitted diseases. Especially vulnerable in this house are Sun trigram people.

The Northeast-Facing House:

NORTHEAST-FACING HOUSE, BUILT BETWEEN 1864–1883

- **Period 1** returns 2044–2063
- Flying Stars in the Center: 7–4
- Occupant could be a creative person, but who is under pressure. This could be a writer who struggles to make a living by their creative talent. There could also be love triangles and deception in relationships. This house would be especially hard for the person born under the Sun trigram.

NORTHEAST-FACING HOUSE, BUILT BETWEEN 1884–1903

- **Period 2** returns 2064–2083
- Flying Stars in the Center: 8–5
- Occupants may suffer from problems related to the bones, muscles, hands, and fingers. It can also include arthritis or general aches and pains. Especially vulnerable are people who are the Ken trigram. Children in this house can be under a lot of pressure from parents, school, or self-induced. This is one of those house types in a People Lock Phase from 2004–2023.

NORTHEAST-FACING HOUSE, **BUILT BETWEEN 1904–1923**

● **Period 3** returns 2084–2103

● Flying Stars in the Center: 9–6

● In this house, the father figure or man of the house could have a lot of pressure on him. There could be undermining circumstances for his power and authority both at home and at work. This house type would be especially hard on a person of the Chien trigram. Anyone in this house could have upper body ailments (head and lung region). This house could be bad for a smoker not inclined to quit.

NORTHEAST-FACING HOUSE, **BUILT BETWEEN 1924–1943**

● **Period 4** returns 2104–2123

● Flying Stars in the Center: 1–7

● This is the kind of house where a woman can be deceived in relationships or business. It is also a house type that can encourage addictive behaviors. Not a good house type for someone struggling with their addictions or trying to maintain some kind of twelve-step program. Aside from drugs, cigarettes, and alcohol, people display others addictive behaviors that are not limited to but can include: pornography, gambling, excessive time on the Internet, eBay auctions, abuse of food, and collecting strange things.

A client of mine shared a house with her boyfriend, and he appeared to have an obsession with macabre items such as collecting dentures, skulls, operation tools, and snake skins. He was also a heavy drinker.

NORTHEAST-FACING HOUSE, **BUILT BETWEEN 1944–1963**

● **Period 5** returns 2124–2143

● Flying Stars in the Center: 2–8

● This is a house type where the people can be wealthy but not healthy. They could also be wealthy but lonely. In the Period 8 cycle, occupants need to hear and see circulating water in order to continue to enjoy the good prosperity potential of this house.

NORTHEAST-FACING HOUSE, BUILT BETWEEN 1964–1983

- **Period 6** returns 2144–2163
- Flying Stars in the Center: 3–9
- The energy in the center of this house implies that the occupants will attract legal problems, gossip, robbery, or arguments at the very least. At the same time, this is not a bad house for someone in the law profession. I lived in this house type for about five years and during most of that time I was blissfully unaware that other feng shui practitioners were gossiping about me. During the late 1990s, when feng shui was at the peak of its "trendiness" in Los Angeles, I later came to find out that some other practitioners couldn't stand the fact that I was so busy and well known. Once I received a phone call from a woman who had just attended a business-networking function. She told me that So-and-So had such terrible things to say about me, she figured I was probably a really great feng shui consultant and she hired me. In other words, she saw right through the unwarranted slander campaign. Remember, Newton's Third Law: For every action there is a reaction—equal and opposite. I also use myself as an example here because when a person is in a good personal phase of their life, the negative potential of a house could manifest in very minor ways, such as the annoyance I just described.

NORTHEAST-FACING HOUSE, BUILT BETWEEN 1984–2003

- **Period 7** returns 2164–2183
- Flying Stars in the Center: 4–1
- The occupants in this house can be highly creative people, such as actors, artists, writers, and musicians, or people who are gifted in the fields of academia, politics, advertising, publishing, and the food or fashion industries. It is also very sexual energy that can get people into trouble with infidelity and scandals. For certain people, they can transmute this energy into spiritual energy. This happens to be one of my all-time favorite house types, as long as the rooms are situated in the best possible locations. I lived in this house type for eighteen months and met too many men during that time frame.

NORTHEAST-FACING HOUSE, **BUILT BETWEEN 2004–2023**

● **Period 8** returns 2184–2203

● Flying Stars in the Center: 5–2

● The energy at the center of this house type can be very volatile and negative, triggering major health problems, arguments, or accidents. This energy could unfortunately become very real if the center of the house is an active area, as described (such as a bathroom, staircase, or kitchen.) At the same time, this could be a good house type with careful space planning. I have been helping a number of clients design and build this particular house type; see Chapter Eight regarding the best arrangement of rooms.

NORTHEAST-FACING HOUSE, **BUILT BETWEEN 1844–1863**

● **Period 9** returns 2024–2043

● Flying Stars in the Center: 6–3

● When this house gets built in the next Period 9 cycle or if it is a previous Period 9 house (built between 1844–1863), the energy in the center is somewhat neutral. It is a combination of two energies that are considered worn out and exhausted by the current time frame. In other words, in any given Period 9, the 6 and 3 Flying Stars are very weak. But there is still a potential for problems with the law, the government, military, or just plain arguments. This house could be especially hard on people of the Chen trigram.

The East-Facing House:

EAST-FACING HOUSE, **BUILT BETWEEN 1864–1883**

● **Period 1** returns 2044–2063

● Flying Stars in the Center: 3–8

● Like other house types already described, this house is currently in a Money Lock phase in the Period 8 cycle. This means that the energy in the center of the house indicates there is potential for the occupants to make money, but it is being hampered during the Period 8 cycle (2004–2023) unless the property has an abundant flow of water features. In *Feng Shui for Skeptics*, I teach the formula for figuring out if your house is, has been, or will be in a Locked phase in the future. Even though this house type is in the twenty-year Money Lock from 2004 through 2023, the occupant does have potential to be wealthy, especially in areas related to law or politics.

EAST-FACING HOUSE, **BUILT BETWEEN 1884–1903**

- **Period 2** returns 2064–2083
- Flying Stars in the Center: 4–9
- The occupants in this house can be very artistic and creative, and produce children who are attractive and precocious. Although we don't have a large number of homes this old in Los Angeles, the energy in the center could certainly support someone in the entertainment industry.

EAST-FACING HOUSE, **BUILT BETWEEN 1904–1923**

- **Period 3** returns in 2084–2103
- Flying Stars in the Center: 5–1
- The occupants in this house can have health problems related to the water or fluid systems of the body, such as the kidneys, blood, and circulation. There can also be problems with the prostate, edema, misdiagnosis and/or receiving the wrong medication. In some cases it can indicate an occupant has a potential for taking or abusing drugs.

EAST-FACING HOUSE, **BUILT BETWEEN 1924–1943**

- **Period 4** returns 210—2123
- Flying Stars in the Center: 6–2
- The people in this house can be interested in spirituality, somewhat lonely or aloof, or just very selective about their friends. I have talked to a lot of people in this house type and they often relate how they used to have a more active social life, but became a little more reclusive after living in this house type. There is also a potential for people in this house type to be taken advantage of by a priest or guru-type.

Regarding health matters, there is a potential for problems with the upper body, head, and lung region. This could include headaches or respiratory problems. One memorable client who was a smoker lived in this kind of a house. He really wanted to know what remedies could lessen the likelihood of having lung problems, but told me flat out that he would not quit smoking. So often people just match their house.

EAST-FACING HOUSE, **BUILT BETWEEN 1944–1963**

- **Period 5** returns 2124–2143
- Flying Stars in the Center: 7–3
- In this house type there is potential for robbery or break-in, legal hassles, and bickering. (**See note at end of this chapter about the "robbery" energy.) It could be especially hard on people born to the Chen trigram and exacerbate the potential for a Chen person to have problems with the feet, throat, or nervous system.

EAST-FACING HOUSE, **BUILT BETWEEN 1964–1983**

Period 6 returns 2144–2163

- Flying Stars in the Center: 8-4
- There are two very predictable aspects to this house type: the occupants can have fertility problems and/or there can be problems with the occupant's bones or muscles. This house type could be especially hard on a person of the Ken trigram. This house type is in a twenty-year People Lock from 2004 through 2023, creating an even stronger tendency for fertility problems. Of course, if the occupants in this house type have no desire for children, then it is a moot point.

EAST-FACING HOUSE, **BUILT BETWEEN 1984–2003**

- **Period 7** returns 2164–2183
- Flying Stars in the Center: 9–5
- This house has energy in the center that is undermining for high-risk financial ventures. We say it is bad for stocks and investments. It would be a bad house for a stockbroker to live in. For others, they should just keep their stocks and investments very conservative. It is also a house type where there could be problems with accidents or setbacks in life. I have had a number of clients with this kind of house and what com-

pounded their problems included having a stove in the very center of the house.

The interpretations of the center stars is focused mostly on the "mountain" and "water" stars, but when the Period Star is included, it adds even more meaning. The 9–5 with a 7 Period Star in the center also means the occupant is vulnerable to a surgery in certain years. This house type could be especially hard for a Li trigram person.

EAST-FACING HOUSE, **BUILT BETWEEN 2004–2023**

- **Period 8** returns 2184–2203
- Flying Stars in the Center: 1–6 (with Period 8 Star in center)
- This house has a trilogy (1–6–8) of Flying Stars in the center, which is very promising. It indicates that the occupants have good potential to be prosperous and happy, and able to have lots of kids. What is critical about this house type is that there are areas (such as the center) that are very positive and other areas that spell disaster. The actual floor plan in this house type will make all the difference in how well the occupants do. Review this house type in the following section about the Period 8 Houses.

EAST-FACING HOUSE, **BUILT BETWEEN 1844–1863**

- **Period 9** returns 2024–2043
- Flying Stars in the Center: 2–7
- When this house gets built in the next Period 9 cycle, the energy in the center will have a real mixed message. The owner could be a very righteous person who owns a lot of land, but there could be deceptions and betrayals with which to continuously deal. In the current Period 8 cycle, this house (from 1844–1863) can mean the occupant may have sickness related to the teeth, mouth, lips, jaw, or breasts. I have documented numerous times that clients with the 2–7 energy in an important part of the house, if not the center, have had to deal with breast cancer.

The Southeast-Facing House:

SOUTHEAST-FACNG HOUSE, **BUILT BETWEEN 1864–1883**

- **Period 1** returns 2044–2063
- Flying Stars in the Center: 2–9
- The forces in the middle indicate an occupant could have mental or intellectual challenges. In fact, it is not a good house to conceive children in because they could be born with Down Syndrome. It also means the occupants could be very lonely, have numerous miscarriages, or accidents or illness with lots of bleeding.

I once did a consultation for a man where the 2–9 energy was not in the center of the house, but located in his son's bedroom. I knew that his son was very intelligent, so I just commented on how they beat the odds since this Flying Star combination can undermine intelligence. He then told me that it was weird I should say that since he and his son were part of a volunteer group that played basketball on a regular basis with mentally challenged kids.

I then asked him if his gifted son ever played with matches, and he was shocked because he had recently caught him in his room burning pieces of paper. A more obscure interpretation of the 2–9 combination includes someone playing with fire.

SOUTHEAST-FACING HOUSE, **BUILT BETWEEN 1884–1903**

- **Period 2** returns 2064–2083
- Flying Stars in the Center: 3–1
- In this kind of house the occupants could be argumentative at the very least. The worst-case scenarios involve a house that can attract crime or prostitution. The energy in the very center creates gossip as well. Advanced practitioners can look closely at the whole chart for this house type and see that in other sections the Flying Stars show a pattern where the "female" trigrams (K'un, Sun, Tui, and Li) are in a domination cycle with other trigrams, contributing to more potential problems for a woman in this house.

SOUTHEAST-FACING HOUSE, **BUILT BETWEEN 1904–1923**

- **Period 3** returns 2084–2103
- Flying Stars in the Center: 4–2
- The energy in the center of this house can be benign or illicit, depending on the person living there. The Flying Stars indicate that the man could attract a lot of women in his life. It could be a man with a lot of girlfriends. This could be fine and a lot of fun for the man if he is single and open about his activities. For a married couple, it might undermine their commitment. Often, I am meeting just with the wife and I ask her if her husband is considered handsome and charismatic. The answer is always yes, and sometimes there is eye rolling to signal that infidelity is a potential or has been a past problem in the relationship.

I have also seen this same type of energy work in favor of men who simply had a lot of women in their lives, without the infidelity problem. This included cosmetic surgeons, gynecologists, jewelers, and owners of businesses whose customers were primarily women. It can also include male spiritual teachers who may find it very challenging to have so many adoring female students. This 4–2 combination can also work on behalf of gay men being charming and charismatic to other gay men.

SOUTHEAST-FACING HOUSE, **BUILT BETWEEN 1924–1943**

- **Period 4** returns 2104–2123
- Flying Stars in the Center: 5–3
- Those who dwell in this house may experience problems with their feet, throat, liver, or nervous systems. They may also have ongoing ailments that change yearly or monthly. The people we refer to as hypochondriacs (always some physical complaint) may have a legitimate feng shui excuse! This could also be a house where the eldest son is irritable or accident-prone.

SOUTHEAST-FACING HOUSE, **BUILT BETWEEN 1944–1963**

- **Period 5** returns 2124–2143
- Flying Stars in the Center: 6–4
- This house could have occupants who are very talented in some cre-

ative profession, but the energy in the center of the house is a bit under-mining. It could also produce low back or leg problems for any of the occupants, especially a Sun trigram person. Another way to look at the stars in the center is for the family members they represent. For in-stance, 6 is the father and 4 is the eldest daughter, so there could be problems with that kind of relationship or power struggles with the father and daughter.

SOUTHEAST-FACING HOUSE, BUILT BETWEEN 1964–1983

- **Period 6** returns 2144-2163
- Flying Stars in the Center: 7-5
- This house could have occupants who argue a lot or injure them-selves. There could also be problems related to the teeth, mouth, jaw, chest muscles, or breasts. People who are the Tui trigram could be espe-cially vulnerable and anyone who lives here could be the victim of periodic betrayals, deception, or embezzlement. (Refer to the end of the chapter regarding the "robbery" energy.)

SOUTHEAST-FACING HOUSE, BUILT BETWEEN 1984–2003

- **Period 7** returns 2164–2183
- Flying Stars in the Center: 8–6
- This house type has very sublime energy in the center, whereby the occupants always have potential to be happy and powerful. No particu-lar health problem is indicated, although this house type happens to be in a People Lock phase in the current Period 8 cycle. Water features are a necessity for this house type.

- Regarding houses that are in the twenty-year-locked phases, you can think of the good energy in the center as being trapped. Although water is extremely effective in releasing this trapped energy, an open floor plan can also help considerably. An example of an open floor plan would be if the occupants could walk into the house and make a straight path to the very center of the house without being blocked by any walls.

SOUTHEAST-FACING HOUSE, **BUILT BETWEEN 2004–2023**

- **Period 8** returns 2184–2203

- Flying Stars in the Center: 9–7

- In this house type there is potential for betrayal or deceptions, personally or professionally. There is also a potential for health problems related to the mouth and chest regions. In certain years there could be compounding influences that make occupants prone to attracting a sexually transmitted disease or having surgery.

SOUTHEAST-FACING HOUSE, **BUILT BETWEEN 1844–1863**

- **Period 9** returns 2024–2043

- Flying Stars in the Center: 1–8

- When this house gets built in Period 9, the energies in the center will be very positive. They will be considered excellent for wealth potential, although there is also a tendency toward health problems related to the fluid systems of the body. People living in other countries outside the United States may have a higher chance of living in a structure that is from the last Period 9 cycle (1844–1863). This is a house type that will become "revived" in the next Period 9. But it is also in a Money Locked phase in the current Period 8. There is a necessity for visible, audible water as a vital main remedy for this house type.

The first half of this section has discussed four different house orientations (north-, northeast-, east-, and southeast-facing) throughout nine different construction cycles. The second half of this section will identify the other four house orientations (south-, southwest-, west-, and northwest-facing) throughout the nine different construction cycles.

There will be some similarities between the house types in this section and the following section. For instance, the south-facing houses will have the same Flying Stars in the center as the north-facing houses. The order of the stars will be transposed, but the meanings will often be similar or nearly identical. For example, the north-facing house built in Period 1 has 5–6 in the center and the south-facing house built in Period 1 has 6–5 in the center.

There is a lot of similarity between the interpretation of 5–6 or 6–5. The number on the left side of the dash is called the "mountain star" and the number on the right side is called the "water star." Usually the mountain star relates to health and relationships and the water star relates to money or career. Sometimes, however, they are interchangeable and have almost the same meaning as combinations of energies.

If you are not familiar with the number combinations, do not worry. It is really not necessary to understand the numbers in depth in order to identify your house type and its inherent personality. You only need to know when your house was built and what direction it faces to locate your own house in this chapter and read a little bit about it.

The South-Facing House:

SOUTH-FACING HOUSE, **BUILT BETWEEN 1864–1883**

- **Period 1** returns 2044–2063
- Flying Stars in the Center: 6–5
- Potential health problems related to the upper body or head region can occur with those living here. This house is not good for a man over age sixty because it can undermine his health or his authority. This house can be especially hard for occupants who are the Chien trigram.

SOUTH-FACING HOUSE, **BUILT BETWEEN 1884–1903**

- **Period 2** returns 2064–2083
- Flying Stars in the Center: 7–6
- Although this house may be good for people involved in police work or self-defense, for most people it can contribute to arguments and even assault or injury from metal objects. Positioned in a crime-ridden neighborhood, this could be the house where the occupants are either the victims or perpetrators of gang violence.

SOUTH-FACING HOUSE, **BUILT BETWEEN 1904–1923**

- **Period 3** returns 2084–2103
- Flying Stars in the Center: 8–7
- This house is in a twenty-year People Lock from 2004 through 2023.

This could undermine fertility or the health of the occupants in general. This house was also in a twenty-year Money Lock from 1984 through 2003. Sometimes the twenty-year Locked phases can be consecutive, such as in this house type.

SOUTH-FACING HOUSE, **BUILT BETWEEN 1924–1943**

- **Period 4** returns 2104–2123
- Flying Stars in the Center: 9–8
- This house will be in a twenty-year Money Lock from 2004 through 2023. As with all houses in a Locked phase, there needs to be generous amounts of audible and visible water on the premises to cure this long-term problem. This house will go into a twenty-year People Lock in 2024.

SOUTH-FACING HOUSE, **BUILT BETWEEN 1944–1963**

- **Period 5** returns 2124–2143
- Flying Stars in the Center: 1–9
- Li trigram people are the most vulnerable in this house because the 1–9 combination is a clash of water dominating fire and Li is the fire trigram. There is a potential heart of eye problems for the occupants, as well as fire-related accidents.

SOUTH-FACING HOUSE, **BUILT BETWEEN 1964–1983**

- **Period 6** returns 2144–2163
- Flying Stars in the Center: 2–1
- In this house the woman needs to be heard and have power, and there is a tendency for the woman to be too strong for the man. There can easily be a separation. I have a few clients who are surviving this house as married couples. In each case the husband is very secure and easygoing or he admires his wife's capabilities and is not threatened by them. When I have a single female client in this house type, I encourage her to find a boyfriend who is sweet and not macho. It is also important for her to use the peach blossom romance remedy highlighted in Chapter Six. That way she can increase her chances of attracting a man in a house that normally undermines romance.

SOUTH-FACING HOUSE, **BUILT BETWEEN 1984–2003**

- **Period 7** returns 2164–2183
- Flying Stars in the Center: 3–2
- This house always presents the potential for legal problems, accidents, and arguments. It is even more conclusive when the important rooms in the house fall in the negative zones. This is the kind of house where the floor plan inside can either help compensate for the center or make it much worse.

SOUTH-FACING HOUSE, **BUILT BETWEEN 2004–2023**

- **Period 8** returns 2184–2203
- Flying Stars in the Center: 4–3
- The 4–3 center indicates that an occupant can be highly intelligent or creative, but also prone to having arguments or gossip in their personal or professional life. There is even a chance for some kind of affair or sexual indiscretion with which to deal.

SOUTH-FACING HOUSE, **BUILT BETWEEN 1844–1863**

- **Period 9** returns 2024–2043
- Flying Stars in the Center: 5–4
- The 5 Star likes to irritate whatever it is around and the 4 Star is associated with the lower part of the body. Occupants in this house could have any number of problems with the lower back, legs, hips, thighs, or knees. There is also a chance for rheumatism or skin problems.

The Southwest-Facing House:

SOUTHWEST-FACING HOUSE, **BUILT BETWEEN 1864–1883**

- **Period 1** returns 2044–2063
- Flying Stars in the Center: 4–7
- The occupant could be very creative but held back in his or her creative profession. It is also possible for there to be pain or injuries with the legs. And on a whole other level, the 4 Star represents the eldest

daughter and the 7 Star represents the youngest daughter so it could reveal a sibling rivalry between two sisters.

SOUTHWEST-FACING HOUSE, **BUILT BETWEEN 1884–1903**

- **Period 2** returns 2064–2083
- Flying Stars in the Center: 5–8
- In this house the 5 Star is going to irritate the 8 Star, which represents the bones and muscles. The occupants could have skeletal or muscular problems including arthritis. The youngest son in the house could also feel tremendous pressure and be accident-prone.

SOUTHWEST-FACING HOUSE, **BUILT BETWEEN 1904–1923**

- **Period 3** returns 2084–2103
- Flying Stars in the Center: 6–9
- A person dwelling in this house could suffer upper body and head region problems, and everything from allergies, sinus problems, headaches, or more serious ailments in the upper body region. The father or man in the house will be under pressure and may not have the respect of the other family members.

SOUTHWEST-FACING HOUSE, **BUILT BETWEEN 1924–1943**

- **Period 4** returns 2104–2123
- Flying Stars in the Center: 7–1
- This 7–1 combination has been discussed in a couple areas of the book, with the common interpretation being that the 7–1 Stars can encourage addictive behaviors. It is also a possibility that the woman in this house is very attractive and could look younger than her age. She may be a "clothes horse" or just very fashion conscious with a big wardrobe. I have had clients who stored their liquor in the 7–1 part of the house. I have also had female clients in this house type who turned a spare bedroom into a walk-in closet to accommodate all their clothing.

SOUTHWEST-FACING HOUSE, **BUILT BETWEEN 1944–1963**

- **Period 5** returns 2124–2143
- Flying Stars in the Center: 8–2
- This house is in a People Lock from 2004 through 2023, where water on the property is needed to alleviate this phase, which can sabotage getting pregnant or activate other health problems.

SOUTHWEST-FACING HOUSE, **BUILT BETWEEN 1964–1983**

- **Period 6** returns 2144–2163
- Flying Stars in the Center: 9–3
- Whenever there is a 3 in the center of a house (combined with any other number) the occupant can attract legal problems, arguments, bickering, gossip, and theft. This particular house has a number of redeeming features, however, and the floor plan inside this house type will greatly determine whether or not those legal problems will be minor or serious.

SOUTHWEST-FACING HOUSE, **BUILT BETWEEN 1984–2003**

- **Period 7** returns 2164–2183
- Flying Stars in the Center: 1–4
- This is one of my favorite house types and the occupants can be very creative, artistic, musical, academic, and social. Some of my most creative clients have naturally gravitated toward this house type.

SOUTHWEST-FACING HOUSE, **BUILT BETWEEN 2004–2023**

- **Period 8** returns 2184–2203
- Flying Stars in the Center: 2–5
- If you have read through all the house types and the individual meanings of the 2 and 5 Stars, you can imagine that this "dynamic duo" is not at all auspicious when it lands in the center of the house. This combination can point to potential disasters and major health problems. The good news is that when two lousy numbers wind up in the center of a house, it means there is *less* negativity in other parts of the house. Every single house has the 2 and 5 Stars paired up twice with some

other number, so if a 2 and 5 are in the center, it mathematically means that the more positive numbers are likely to be in the bedrooms and entrances. A carefully planned floor plan for this house can still produce a good house.

SOUTHWEST-FACING HOUSE, **BUILT BETWEEN 1844–1863**

● **Period 9** returns 2024–2043

● Flying Stars in the Center: 3–6

● There is a possibility in this house for the father to be very strict with the son and maybe even overbearing. The occupants could have problems with their feet, throat, or nervous systems. This could include speech problems, such as stuttering.

The West-Facing House:

WEST-FACING HOUSE, **BUILT BETWEEN 1864–1883**

● **Period 1** returns 2044–2063

● Flying Stars in the Center: 8–3

● The 8–3 combination can indicate fertility problems, especially during Period 8 when the house is in a 20–year People Lock. The occupants could also have deformities or pains with the bones, muscles, hands, and fingers.

WEST-FACING HOUSE, **BUILT BETWEEN 1884–1903**

● **Period 2** returns 2064–2083

● Flying Stars in the Center: 9–4

● A person living in this house can be highly creative and artistic. He or she can be very charismatic also, in either a sexual way or a spiritual way, or both. This could also be the home of a writer or public speaker.

WEST-FACING HOUSE, **BUILT BETWEEN 1904–1923**

● **Period 3** returns 2084–2103

● Flying Stars in the Center: 1–5

● Something can go wrong in this house with the occupant's blood, circulation, ears, kidneys, or any fluid systems of the body. This could include impotency. It is easy for an occupant to be misdiagnosed and be given the wrong medication. If other negative feng shui features are also in force, this could be the home of someone who takes or deals drugs.

WEST-FACING HOUSE, **BUILT BETWEEN 1924–1943**

- **Period 4** returns 2104–2123
- Flying Stars in the Center: 6–2
- The Chien and K'un trigrams represent an older man and an older woman, which can also symbolize a priest and a nun. This gives way to an implication that the occupant could be taken advantage of by a religious leader. Some of these definitions of the center of the house may not be relevant, such as the case of a person living in this house who is not involved in an organized religion or blindly following a guru-type. But it is always very interesting to find out about what happened to past occupants whenever possible. The 6–2 combination can make anyone a bit of a loner however.

WEST-FACING HOUSE, **BUILT BETWEEN 1944–1963**

- **Period 5** returns 2124–2143
- Flying Stars in the Center: 3–7
- Because the 3 indicates a legal dispute and the 7 can attract betrayals, this "robbery star combination" can attract some really surprising situations, such as being betrayed by a trusted friend or relative. There can be legal entanglements that seem to come out of nowhere. I have lived in this house type and sometimes bizarre things would happen. For instance, I once found out by accident that a person was selling pirated copies of my feng shui videos on eBay. (A cease and desist letter had to be sent out.) Copyright infringement falls under the category of what I call the "gentlemen's robbery."

WEST-FACING HOUSE, **BUILT BETWEEN 1964–1983**

● **Period 6** returns 2144–2163

● Flying Stars in the Center 4–8

● Here the occupants have potential to be prosperous but there is a Money Lock on this house during Period 8, so water is needed to release this stifling lock. If this is your house, go back to Chapter Four to review the best locations to place water outside your property.

WEST-FACING HOUSE, **BUILT BETWEEN 1984–2003**

● **Period 7** returns 2164–2183

● Flying Stars in the Center: 5–9

● The 5 Star indicates setbacks and delays or accidents and arguments. The 9 Star just intensifies this. It is important for this house to have a good floor plan in every other way to compensate for the center. A totally nonobvious symptom of the 5–9 center is that it is not a good house for someone to take risks with stocks and investments.

WEST-FACNG HOUSE, **BUILT BETWEEN 2004–2023**

● **Period 8** returns 2184–2203

● Flying Stars in the Center: 6–1

● Even though all the numbers go through their positive and negative cycles (over a 180-year span), the 6 Star and the 1 Star are considered inherently good most of the time. The 6 Star is considered weak during the Period 8, but this combination still suggests the occupants could be powerful and affluent.

WEST-FACING HOUSE, **BUILT BETWEEN 1844–1863**

● **Period 9** returns 2024–2043

● Flying Stars in the Center: 7–2

● Since the 2 Star can bring sickness to whatever number it is combined with, the 7 Star can make occupants vulnerable to problems with the teeth, mouth, lips, tongue, jaw, and chest.

There could also an episode of depression in response to being betrayed or assaulted. In certain years, this house is prone to a fire.

The Northwest-Facing House:

NORTHWEST-FACING HOUSE, **BUILT BETWEEN 1864–1883**

- **Period 1** returns 2044–2063
- Flying Stars in the Center: 9–2
- A person in this house runs the risk of being sick, having mental imbalances, and bleeding accidents. It is also a house where there could be miscarriages.

NORTHWEST-FACING HOUSE, **BUILT BETWEEN 1884–1903**

- **Period 2** returns 2064–2083
- Flying Stars in the Center: 1–3
- Gossip in the entertainment industry sometimes catapults a person into more wealth and work opportunities. But since most human beings on this planet are not entertainers, this 3 Star could easily instigate harmful gossip, arguments, or thievery. The 3 Star in the center of the house could make someone the victim of or the perpetrator of a crime if compounding negative features are also in place.

NORTHWEST-FACING HOUSE, **BUILT BETWEEN 1904–1923**

- **Period 3** returns 2084–2103
- Flying Stars in the Center: 2–4
- If a single man lives in this house, he can be very charismatic to women and most likely have numerous opportunities for relationships. For a woman in this house, she could be cheated on, whether the man lives in this house with her or not. Since the 2 Star represents the mother and the 4 Star represents the eldest daughter, there is a nonobvious symptom that a mother and daughter will not get along or even a mother-in-law and daughter-in-law will not get along.

NORTHWEST-FACING HOUSE, **BUILT BETWEEN 1924–1943**

- **Period 4** returns 2104–2123
- Flying Stars in the Center: 3–5
- Occupants could have ongoing, changing health problems. People who are the Chen trigram are most vulnerable in this house type. Since the 3 Star is also associated with thunder and lightning, an obscure possibility is that the occupant or their house could be struck by lightning. I have also had clients whose homes were struck by lightning when there was an annual 3 or monthly 3 in the location of where the lightning struck.

NORTHWEST-FACING HOUSE, **BUILT BETWEEN 1944–1963**

- **Period 5** returns 2124–2143
- Flying Stars in the Center: 4–6
- Low back or leg problems could plague an occupant in this house type. A person who is the Sun trigram is most likely to be affected by this. When someone knows there is a potential for a certain problem because of their house, they can seek out a comprehensive analysis, but also be proactive in their lifestyle and habits to prevent such situations. Someone in this house type might need to be cautious that they do not engage in types of exercises that would risk back injury or keep their low back in shape with regular chiropractic treatment.

NORTHWEST-FACING HOUSE, **BUILT BETWEEN 1964–1983**

- **Period 6** returns 2144–2163
- Flying Stars in the Center: 5–7
- This house was in a twenty-year Money Lock from 1984–2003. If you have lived in this house during and after this period, you could easily have noticed the improvement in finances post 2004. The 7 Star is related to the breasts. Men get breast cancer, not just women, so that is one of the more serious indications emanating from the center of this house. Less likely to be life-threatening but still capable of causing a tremendous amount of aggravation could be a botched breast enlargement surgery. Tui women are the most vulnerable in this scenario.

NORTHWEST-FACING HOUSE, BUILT BETWEEN 1984–2003

● **Period** 7 returns 2164–2183

● Flying Stars in the Center: 6–8

● This is one of the few houses that have such a positive center. The potential to do well financially is there, but in Period 8 the house has a Money Lock to damper the great potential. If this house had a very open floor plan and was right on the beach, it would likely not experience the Locked phase and be just fine.

NORTHWEST-FACING HOUSE, BUILT BETWEEN 2004–2023

● **Period** 8 returns 2184–2203

● Flying Stars in the Center: 7–9

● Often, a feng shui audit is amazingly specific. But there is also a wide range of meanings for some of these number combinations and we are only reviewing the center stars in this chapter, not the entire house. The 7–9 combination could indicate something as minor as dental problems to something as major as being assaulted or betrayed on a grand scale.

If you are the Tui trigram, this house could put a lot of pressure on you.

NORTHWEST-FACING HOUSE, BUILT BETWEEN 1844–1863

● **Period** 9 returns 2024–2043

● Flying Stars in the Center: 8–1

● During any Period 9 cycle, the 8–1 Stars are very positive in their respective definitions as prosperity stars. Still, there is a domination cycle going on here that should be examined. The 8 Star (earth) will dominate the 1 Star (water), so there is a chance for the occupants to have "water-related" problems: kidneys, blood, circulation, ears, and glands in general. A K'an trigram person in this house would be most vulnerable.

The Flying Stars are the trigrams. Whenever the stars in the center of the house match the personal trigrams of the actual occupants, it further activates the hidden agenda. If a Ken trigram person and a K'an trigram person were living in this house type, they would have more conflicts and power struggles than people of different trigrams.

A Word About the "Robbery" Energy

In a number of house-type descriptions, I have indicated that the occupants could be prone to robbery or legal problems. I know that when I am consulting in person with a client, the words "robbery" can conjure up images of being assaulted, having one's house broken into, and being robbed by a stranger. While this can in fact happen, I have also noted a lot of other "creative" ways that people get robbed that are not life-threatening or perpetrated by a stranger.

I call this the "gentleman's robbery," such as when your mortgage broker overcharges you in a real estate transaction. Your stockbroker could be reckless with your portfolio, you could be the victim of identify theft, credit card fraud, or even just an overzealous parking enforcement officer needing to meet his daily quota. The robbery energy could involve any legal document or situation with legal consequences. Whether it is taxes, insurance policies, business contracts, custody disputes, or inheritances, everywhere you turn there is an opportunity to be taken advantage of legally and financially.

Some people have that going on in their lives without finding out until after the damage is done. In fact, I have had clients whose family members embezzled from family businesses or spouses who stole money from each other's separate accounts. I have one client who sells antiques over the Internet. Occasionally, buyers try to return fakes to him and ask for their money back. After being taken advantage of a couple of times, he now signs the antiques with invisible ink before sending them out, so if a fake piece gets returned to him, he has proof of it.

Pick Your Poison

After reading through the list of potential problems for various house types, it may seem like almost all of them are "accidents waiting to happen." The beauty of feng shui is that there are often remedies for these hidden negative potentials. Feng shui masters debate about whether or not you can really change the energy of the center of the house. Unlike the other directional sections, the energies in the center are not really confined to the literal center of the house.

At the same time, I would say that *if* your center is not just a pass through area, but an actual room or part of a room that you spend time in, then it would be appropriate to apply Five-Element Theory to the center of that house. The only reason I have not listed the remedy for the center of the house is because it would be a bit reckless of me to do so without knowing more about your actual house. Also, there are yearly influences that come to the center of every house that can have an overriding or contradictory effect.

You would need a deeper understanding of the Flying Stars in order to tackle the energy in the center of your house. Or you should find a competent consultant who can look at your property as a whole.

In listing the hidden potential (center energy) of these house types, the goal is not to scare you or make you feel like practically every house is lousy. But if something in the description rings true for you about your own house and it has been a nagging or serious problem, then you might actually consider getting a comprehensive analysis to determine whether or not it is worth staying in that house. I even divulged some of the house types I have lived in, so you can better appreciate that no one is exempt from having at least occasional problems and no house is perfect.

The bottom line is that some aspects of a house's personality can change and some cannot. You are becoming familiar with these number patterns. There are nine numbers and they are paired up with each other to create eighty-one different number combinations. You have been introduced to seventy-two different number patterns that can exist in the center of a house. The remaining nine combinations do not occur in the center of the house (as mountain and water stars), such as 1–1, 2–2, 3–3, and so forth. But those doubled up number patterns do exist in other parts of certain house types.

In addition to the eighty-one different Flying Star combinations, these energies behave uniquely depending on where they are located. For instance, a 3–8 combination behaves differently in the northeast part of the house than the southeast part of a house. Each of the eight basic directions has its own special influence on the number patterns. Add the annual stars into each directional quadrant and you have quite a math puzzle to decipher.

CHAPTER EIGHT

If These Walls Could Talk

Who Moved My Ch'i?

In modern times, we have the ability to move houses. There is nothing written about moved houses in the ancient Chinese feng shui texts. What happens when you move a house? Like an appliance that gets unplugged from the electrical socket, the energy current becomes disconnected. When a house is plopped onto new land, it will fairly quickly reconnect with that new land and absorb the energies of that land, the same as if it had been built there over months of time.

Although I have evaluated thousands of houses, I have only consulted on a couple dozen mobile homes. Most mobile homes are placed on land without any intention of moving them. Even though they are not built in the traditional way, once they are stationed on the land with a specific orientation, they do seem to affect the occupants in the exact same way as if they were a regular house with a raised foundation.

More and more people are opting for prefab houses that are partially or completely constructed off the premises and then moved to the lot as a ready-made house. These should be interpreted just the same as a house that was built on the lot from scratch.

If you have a house that was completely lifted off the ground in order to reinforce the foundation, that house may or may not have taken on a new Flying Star chart. Those rare circumstances need to be treated on a case-by-case basis. Once I received an email from a woman who was trying to figure out if she should recalculate her house since it shifted 5 degrees after an earthquake. It was originally facing southwest 1 and then moved to southwest 2 after the quake. But like a washing machine that might shift a little when the laundry load is out of balance, the house is still "plugged in" to its original location and no recalculations are made. This would be true for any house that shifts a few degrees because of earthquakes.

While exercising on a stationary bike at my health club, I often sat next to an elderly woman who lived in the "Witch's House" of Beverly Hills for thirty-five years. The Witch's House is a somewhat cartoon-looking house with an undulating roof line and brick design that almost appears like a "melting" gingerbread house. It really stands out against the more stately and conservative architecture in the area. We talked often and I learned that the Witch's House was originally built as an office space for the movie studios in Culver City and then was relocated to Beverly Hills years later. With her house as a perfect example, regardless of when it was first built, the new construction date would need to be recalculated based on the year it was moved. The former owner gave me a lot of insight and history into this famous house, which she loved, in spite of having to endure frequent tourists who hoisted themselves on top of those giant Beverly Hills trash cans just to get a glimpse of her backyard. But she loved the house in spite of pesky tourists.

Sometimes a house will be more well known than its occupants. This is something that is understood and documented by feng shui consultants. In fact, I have been to some commercial buildings in Southern California on several different occasions for different occupants and the experiences of these different clients have been similar. In downtown Los Angeles I have gone to the Cooper Building and the Fashion Mart Building numerous times for different clients, and I always marvel at how these two buildings are so appropriate in their Flying Star charts for the fashion industry.

In the *Los Angeles Times,* there was an article printed on April 29, 2005, titled *It Changed Hands—And Hearts.* The article was about a modest house in West Hollywood and the various owners who had lived there over a spread of nearly eighty years. The article was primarily focused on the escalation of its selling price over the decades, but they also noted the careers of the various owners. Out of eleven owners, six of the more recent ones were in the entertainment industry.

I believe houses attract certain similar type people. I once did a consultation in Hermosa Beach for a man who was a successful chef. He confided in me that he used to have an addiction problem but managed to conquer it with the daily practice of yoga. A few years later, I returned to that same house when a new client called me. Just hearing the address on the phone didn't register as familiar to me, but when I approached the house I remembered that I had been there before. I told this client that I had actually been to her house before and she laughed. She said the previous occupant told her what remedies to put in the house, but she didn't know if she could believe him. He told her he did great in the house and left her his garden fountain as a gift. This situation was ironic on several levels. Aside from them calling in the same consultant for the same house, she was a professional yoga teacher who loved to cook in her free time; he was a professional chef who did yoga in his free time.

The High Drama House: Sex, Drugs, and Rock 'n' Roll

I ended up evaluating dozens of homes for one client before he settled on a house that reminded him of the home he grew up in. During the house-hunting phase, he asked me to come over and do a quickie reading on his current house even though he didn't plan on living there much longer. He was just curious about the feng shui he had been living in for the past seventeen years, so he could understand better the influence feng shui could have on him in the next house.

This house in the Hollywood Hills was a really odd shape, like a giant golf ball, clinging to the edge of the mountain. It was even a little challenging doing a compass reading to establish a sitting and facing orientation for a structure with curved exterior walls.

Once I calculated the Flying Star chart for the house, I was able to tell him that it is the kind of house where there can be "high drama," ups and downs, where one year could be great for the occupant and another year could be a disaster. This is actually a fairly common house type and not everybody living in it will experience such extremes from year to year, but the potential is there. In fact, over the years I have seen quite a few entertainment industry people live in this kind of house. When I mention "high drama" or big surprises, creative people just kind of take it in stride. This may be a normal situation for people with careers in entertainment. Not only did this house in the Hollywood Hills present a potential for big surprises, but heavily used areas of the house had the 1–7 energy, which can feed addictions. Referring back to the previous chapter, the house with the 1–7 Flying Stars in the center can trigger or encourage addictive behaviors.

My client was grinning and nodding at that point in the consultation. Right in the 1–7 part of his living room, he told me he'd had a particular chair where he used to administer his drugs. My client had been drug-free for many years when I met him, but he confided that he still went to a daily twelve-step meeting to stay clean and sober, and he too had become a yoga aficionado.

He then confided a little of the house's history: Other occupants of his home had included the late singer Ricky Nelson, legendary Jimi Hendrix, and comedian Sam Kinison. The demise of these famous people did not occur while they lived in this exact same house, yet they were certainly examples of how a person may be consciously or unconsciously attracted to certain house types to fulfill a destiny already written.

The Power of Feng Shui in the Wrong Hands

Most of my clients are wonderful people I enjoy advising and influencing. They are conscious, open-minded beings who are working on themselves and trying to balance their homes to benefit all their family members. But every once in a while I find myself in a situation that is deeply disturbing.

I was consulting with a woman whose master bedroom had pretty bad energy. I began telling her what she could do to improve the space so she and her husband could avoid the inherent health risks of the room. I routinely make it a point to also inform people of what they should *not* do if they do not want to further activate the negative aspects.

Once I was through telling this woman about her bedroom, she confided that she was currently sleeping in the living room on the couch and that she had been sleeping apart from her husband for quite a while since their marriage was on the rocks. She also confirmed that his health was very bad, just as I predicted. I reflexively began to remind her of what she could do and change about the room in order to help him.

It was at that moment that a very sick smile spread across her face and she asked me to please remind her again what *not* to do. Then she winked at me! I stammered a bit because I then realized that she was in fact going to do exactly what I told her *not* to do!
And I had already written down notes for her that I couldn't exactly scratch over.

I had unintentionally given her a recipe to harm her husband. It was very awkward, and I could not have imagined that coming. Years later, I had another client tell me as I was walking out his door that he would love to learn feng shui so he could use it "offensively." I couldn't even bring myself to ask him to elaborate on what he meant.

Although the disturbing consultations are few and far between, they are certainly memorable: A prostitute once picked up my business card at the Bodhi Tree Bookstore and expected me to give her advice to help her money-laundering business. I went to her home before I found out her "occupation"and realized she was quite disturbed. Being in her home was surreal, and the only time I actually became concerned about my physical safety during a consultation.

She had a shrine erected in her bedroom with a giant poster of Brad Pitt, who she insisted would be paying her a visit. "His people" were supposedly talking to "her people." Of course you must be wondering if her house had terrible feng shui or if aspects to it indicated that someone like she would live there.

There was nothing extraordinarily remarkable about the house. It happened to be positioned at the end of a long cul-de-sac, which is a generic feng shui flaw. It was a common house type that is considered bad for money and bad for relationships. This house type benefits from having lower land level behind it and yet she had a steep hill behind her house, which made things even worse. I mentioned this to her just as an aside, and in one comically absurd moment she chimed in that she could get one of her "customers," who was a contractor, to do a "trade-in services" with her. I guess she thought it would be no problem to get him to bring in a tractor and clear the hill behind her house in exchange for a year of sex!

Remember, the law of karma is Newton's Third Law: For every action there is a reaction, equal and opposite. If you use feng shui for destructive purposes, you will have to deal with the fallout eventually. This is one reason why I never recommend those infamous Bagua mirrors. When people hang mirrors to shoot negative energy back at someone, like a neighbor across the street, I can't help but think there will be some kind of unfortunate back lash to follow. There are many remedies for protecting or shielding yourself from oncoming negativity, but to do something that will hurt another person in the process is not my idea of living in harmony or consciousness.

The Sixteen Basic House Types Being Built in Period 8 (2004–2023)

This book was first published near the beginning of the Period 8 Cycle (2004–2023). There are sixteen basic house types or house charts being built in this time frame. Some of them are inherently better than others. They all have positive areas and if any architect, designer, or builder wants to use these house charts for guidance, they will be instrumental in helping create a house that will have positive effects on its occupants for many decades to come.

The sixteen different house types are based on their orientation. What you know to be the facing wall direction of the house will be the direction that defines the house in this chapter. (Once again, we will assume that the facing wall is parallel to the back/sitting wall.) In each house type chart, you will see the directions within the house that are considered positive or at least have good potential.

This is by no means a do-it-yourself evaluation. In fact, you would be wise to obtain the services of an expert to help you perfect these spaces. Some areas have good potential *but still need remedies on an ongoing basis.*

The purpose of this section is to help you set up a house properly in the design phase or to help you in the initial stages of house hunting for houses built between the years of 2004 and 2023. *The positive areas should be saved for entrances, bedrooms, or home offices.* The areas that are not positive should be relegated to bathrooms, storage areas, hallways, or even dining rooms and kitchens.

Use these charts as a house-hunting guide for the ideal floor plans within these various house types. Again, this is not a complete analysis of any of the homes, and you are wise to seek out professional help from a classically trained practitioner to complete the analysis.

Some of the areas that are noted to be "positive" mean they have positive potential, but without a remedy there could definitely be problems. When I say they need a remedy, it is something simple but important such as a water fountain, a metal object, or one of the other elements discussed in previous chapters.

I frequently get calls from clients who want a crash course in what to look for in an ideal home in their house-hunting search. This is extremely difficult to do, but at least these sixteen house types are a beginning guide. *Remember, these houses described are only those built in 2004 through 2023.*

These charts can also be used as guidelines for commercial structures. The same positive areas within each structure could be applied for a business. Place the entrance in one of the most positive areas. Important departments or divisions of the company go in the other positive zones. If you have a business with a sales force, put them in the major prosperity zones to help bring in more business for the company.

These charts can also guide you in your remodel plans. If you do a drastic remodel and virtually gut your existing house, (removing the ceiling and the roof) then it is likely you will be creating totally new ch'i and a new time chart in your house. This will be true if a major portion of your ceiling gets opened up and exposed to the sky.

Another type of remodel is the room addition. If you add on a new room to your house (not enlarging an existing room), then you can consider the room addition to be a mini-house and you can plan where in the new bedroom would be an ideal location for the bed itself.

Important note: Some famous authors have indicated that the ideal house is a Period 8 house during the Period 8 time frame and that older homes are now at a serious disadvantage or harmful to people. I have received emails from people who have been unnecessarily worried about their Period 4, 5, 6, or 7 house types now that we have entered the Period 8. People have gotten the *wrong* impression that they must remodel their homes from other construction cycles to force them into being Period 8 houses. This is not true! Not only is this impractical for most people, it is truly not necessary and by trying to do so, you could be taking a perfectly good house and turning into one of the *unfavorable* Period 8 house types.

For the sixteen Period 8 house types:
The code for understanding how the areas are ranked is as follows:

Pos+ means very positive. Outstanding area for a bedroom, main entrance or other heavily used part of house or building.

Pos means positive. Also a good area to occupy for frequently used rooms. At least some of the energies are positive in these areas or the imbalance would be easy to correct.

Neg means negative. These areas should be used as little as possible because heavy use increases health, relationship, or financial setbacks. This does not mean one should be afraid to step foot in these areas; just make them the less important rooms if you are designing your house to these specifications.

No demarcations in the directional quadrants means it is a so-so location, not terrible but not great, and probably in need of some remedies (metal, water, wood, fire, or earth) to balance it out in the long-term.

The charts included in this section will show the facing side of the house toward the bottom of the page. Look at the charts as if they were an aerial view and know that if the house is not a perfect square, these directional quadrants will take on different shapes.

A rectangular-shaped house will have rectangular shaped quadrants. Some houses may have extensions or missing quadrants. It does take training to know how to place these grids correctly over oddly-shaped houses. You would be wise to enlist the services of a practitioner to help you decipher houses with unusual shapes.

Period 8 House Facing North 1

SE	S	SW
Neg		
E	C	W
Pos		Neg
NE	N	NW
Pos	Pos+	

This is a house type that is considered inherently good for money potential and it would be a shame not to use that north quadrant for something important. Conversely, the southeast and west quadrants in this house present great chance for mishap. This can be averted if these spaces are relegated to minor rooms within the house.

This is a Li House (sits south, facing north) and the most compatible occupants for this house type would be Li, K'an, Chen, or Sun Trigram people.

Period 8 House Facing N2 or 3

SE	S	SW
	Pos+	Pos
E	C	W
Neg		Pos
NE	N	NW
		Neg

This is another Li House type, considered inherently good for the health and relationships of occupants. It could be also supportive for money luck if the master bedroom were positioned in the back south quadrant. Even if the master bedroom were to span across the southeast or southwest quadrants as well, at least the placement of the bed should be in the south.

Period 8 House Facing NE 1

S	SW Pos	W
SE	C Neg	NW Pos
E Pos	NE Pos	N

This house type in general is considered one of the best house types being built in the Period 8 Construction Cycle. There are four areas noted as being positive but they won't get the Pos+ (very positive) ranking without remedies. The very center is quite negative, however, and this should be just a pass-through area. One of my clients began designing a house in 2004 that was destined to be this "Wang Shan Wang Shui" (good for people and good for money) house type, but the shape of the house (missing NE) was going to place the entrance virtually in the center of the house. They followed my recommendations to alter the shape of the house so that they would not be missing the northeast quadrant and the entrance would be in the northeast rather than the center.

This K'un House (sits southwest/faces northeast) is especially good for people in the "west" group according to the East/West School of feng shui. This includes K'un, Ken, Tui, and Chien Trigram people.

Period 8 House Facing NE 2 or 3

S	SW Pos	W Pos
SE Pos	C Neg	NW
E	NE Pos	N

This house type is called a "Reversed House" according Flying Star feng shui and the four major house type divisions. This means there could be both money and health problems. This could be a good house, however, if there are many remedies in place, both inside and outside the house. It is the kind of house that needs a large water feature in back on the SW side, so if you were looking at a house like this with a pool in the back, it will be much better for money luck. Also, if the land level is higher on the front side of the property and/or across the street, then the "virtual mountain" of the higher land level can fix this house and make it better for the occupants' health. This is also good for the west type people.

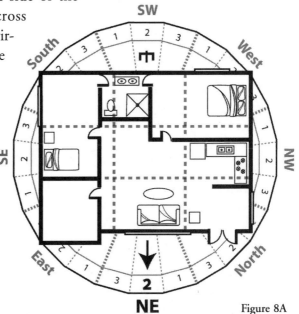

Figure 8A

Period 8 House Facing East 1

SW	W	NW
		Neg
S	C	N
Neg	Pos	Pos
SE	E	NE
	Pos+	

This house type is called Double Facing in Flying Star feng shui and is considered inherently strong for money luck. This could all be sabotaged, however, if important rooms or entrances land in the northwest or south quadrants. These are the two most negative areas of this house type.

Remember, when a house faces east, by definition it "sits" in the west. This house type also caters more to people in the "west" group (Ken, K'un, Tui, Chien).

Period 8 House Facing East 2 or 3

SW	W	MW
	Pos+	
S	C	N
Pos	Pos	Neg
SE	E	NE
Neg		

This house is referred to as Double Sitting, inherently good for the occupant's health and relationships. It can be made better for money potential like other Double Sitting house types, with water such as a fountain or a pool behind it. Careful placement of important areas can also make this a great house.

Period 8 House Facing SE 1

W Neg	NW Pos+	N Neg
SW	C	NE Neg
S	SE Pos+	E Neg

This house is referred to as a Reversed House. All Reversed Houses need water behind them to make them better for money potential, and they all need higher land level or some kind of mountainous energy in front of them to make them better for health and well-being of the occupants. A mountain can be a literal mountain, a taller building, a tree that is higher than the house, a brick wall on the front side, or a hardscape that includes large boulders or potted plants at least several feet high. Obviously, the taller the mountain energy, the more effective it is.

This house could be utilized well if the really important areas were in the positive+ areas. And for two-story houses it is especially lucky if these positive areas on each floor can be used. For example, in this house type, there could be a front door in the southeast, a back door in the northwest, and then even a master bed upstairs in the northwest. This could make a tremendous difference in how well someone does in this house type, along with the proper exterior corrections.

Period 8 House Facing SE 2 or 3

W Neg	NW Pos+	N Neg
SW Neg	C	NE Pos
S Neg	SE Pos+	E Neg

This house type is similar to the other southeast-facing house in that there are more potential negative zones, but it is a slightly better house type in general because of the 15-degree difference in compass alignment. It is one of the four basic house types called "Wang Shan Wang Shui," inherently good for people and good for money.

So if you have some leeway on the orientation of your southeast-facing house, try to make it this one instead of the SE1 house.

Both of these southeast-facing houses (therefore northwest sitting) are especially good for west type people. Both of these southeast-facing houses will enter a twenty-year period called a People Lock beginning in 2024. When the People Lock is in effect, it makes health matters worse and it also undermines fertility. That is why you need to consider how long you want to live in this house type or the likelihood of living in this house type after 2024.

Period 8 House Facing South 1

NW	N Pos+	NE Pos
W Neg	C	E Pos
SW	S	SE Neg

This is a Double Sitting House, inherently better for health and relationships than income potential; however, with the right floor plan, a frequently used back door through the north and/or a master bedroom in the north could help make it very lucky for wealth also.

The house that faces south by definition sits in the north, making it a house type more compatible for the east group people. This caters to people with the personal trigrams of Li, K'an, Chen, and Sun.

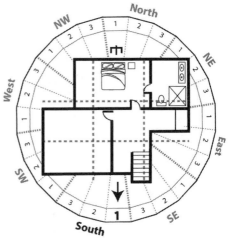

First floor

Figure 8B

Second floor

Period 8 House Facing S2 or 3

NW Neg	N	NE
W Pos	C	E Neg
SW Pos	S Pos+	SE

This is called a Double-Facing House, inherently strong for money luck, but less helpful for relationships or health matters. This house does well with both a mountain and water on the facing side and careful placement of the important rooms in the positive zones is crucial.

Like the previous example, this is also a K'an House (sits north) and best suited for the Li, K'an, Chen, and Sun people.

Period 8 House Facing SW 1

N	NE Pos	E Pos
NW Pos	C Neg	SE
W	SW Pos	S Pos

● This is one of my favorite house types in the Period 8 Construction Cycle, even though the very center is extremely negative. As a basic house type it is Wang Shan Wang Shui and has four positive areas with good potential.

For advanced Flying Star practitioners who want to float all the numbers, it also ends up being a "Combination 10" House, which is another lucky feature to it. As long as the center of the house is kept relatively dormant and not used as a room, this can be a very good house type. Another creative design solution to this house type might be to make a central atrium to the house or building, thus almost eliminating the negative center.

Period 8 House Facing SW 2 or 3

N Pos	NE Pos	E
NW	C Neg	SE Pos
W Pos	SW Pos	S

This is a house type where there can be a lot of unpredictability in both health and finances. My clients in show biz always smile when told this because high drama is a way of life for many of these people. What brings out the worst in any house type is the unfortunate arrangement of rooms within the floor plan as well as the inadvertent use of the wrong colors and elements in the furnishings and decor of those rooms. As an example, the center of this house type should never have any fire in it. If there were a kitchen in the center of this house, it would be like lighting a stick of dynamite in your house every day.

Period 8 House Facing West 1

This is a more unusual house type only in the sense that the center is one of the most positive areas of the whole house. It means there is always potential to do well. As discovered in the previous chapter, the center of most houses is not positive, so this house is more the exception than the rule.

NE	E Pos+	SE
N Pos	C Pos	S Neg
NW Neg	W	SW

These west-facing houses sit in the east, so they cater more to the Li, K'an, Chen, and Sun people.

Period 8 House Facing West 2 or 3

NE	E	SE Neg
N Neg	C Pos	S Pos
NW	W Pos+	SW

This house is the flipped version of the east-facing house at the same degrees of east/west alignment. I have been to countless neighborhoods that were developed all at the same time with "track" housing, meaning the same floor plans for each house. Sometimes they are varied ever so slightly or just the flipped version of the floor plan from the house next to it. When guiding people through house selections in new developments, if they only have one or two floor plan possibilities, I try to see if they can get on the correct side of the street for any given floor plan, to take advantage of where the important rooms are going to land within the floor plan.

Period 8 House Facing NW1

E	SE	S
	Pos+	
NE	C	SW
		Pos
N	NW	W
Neg	Pos+	Neg

In advanced Flying Star feng shui, this house type is called a String of Pearls House. It is not good for an elderly woman or a woman in need of recuperation or recovery from illness. This is also a "Reversed" House type, which means in general there can be money and health problems. This house type would not be considered a good house type compared to other orientation possibilities built in the Period 8 Cycle.

Period 8 House Facing Northwest 2 or 3

E	SE	S
Neg	Pos+	Neg
NE	C	SW
Pos		
N	NW	W
Neg	Pos+	

Just a few degrees away from the other northwest-facing house type just described, this particular northwest-facing house is one of the more promising house types, inherently good for people and money potential.

One circumstance that is true for both northwest-facing house types is that they will both enter into a twenty-year Money Lock (undermining phase for career) beginning in 2024. Take this into consideration as you decide whether or not this is the type of house you want to live in just for a few years or if you want to find a house to live in for decades. If you live in this house type after 2024, it will begin a long-term negative phase in need of more remedies than what would be needed prior to 2024.

How Important Is It to "Match" Your House Type?

Should an "east type" person only live in an "east type" house? Should a "west type" person only live in a "west type" house? The answer is no, but it is one layer of compatibility to consider.

Sitting is the opposite of *facing* and east type houses sit in east, southeast, north and south. They are respectively called the Chen House, Sun House, K'an House, and Li House. West type houses sit in west, southwest, northwest, and northeast. They are respectively called the Tui House, K'un House, Chien House, and Ken House.

The sixteen Period 8 Houses just highlighted do reveal a few house types to be better than others. However, it should also be obvious now that each and every house has positive areas and the right floor plan that takes advantage of these positive zones can be a stable happy home for just about anyone.

The Blueprint for Balanced Living

As members of the human race, we all do some of the same things, have similar experiences, and react predictably. We all eat, but for some of us certain foods are not acceptable while for others those foods are perfectly fine. We have sex, but our approach, attitude, and consciousness toward this activity can partially define who we are as individuals and members (or outcasts) of society.

Some people need rules, laws, and religious codes of conduct in order to make sense of this universe and as reminders to respect other people. Others intuitively know right from wrong and act with compassion even when they don't have to, even when there is no tax deduction as an incentive.

Some people work very hard physically to make their income; others make money with their brain power or through the hard work of employees or some product that "sells itself." And so it goes with building a house, choosing where to live and how we arrange our possessions. The approach and the consciousness toward every aspect of living can vary widely. I have been to homes where I did not feel comfortable drinking the water from the glass that was served to me, and I have been to other homes so immaculate, I could "eat off the floor."

I have had clients who didn't seem to mind or notice really incongruous color combinations on their walls and furnishings while other clients had such sensitivity to color that I had to watch them agonize over choosing between nearly identical shades of white.

With all the information contained in this book, I hope you can use much of it and experience the benefits. But don't worry about circumstances that prevent you from using all the recommendations provided in these pages. Even I cannot take advantage of all the suggestions and powerful tools I know about.

You may also find that some of the recommended directions for your personal trigram will contradict the recommendations based on your Chinese zodiac sign. You may find that a direction which is supposed to be a personal wealth direction is also a draining direction. What would happen if that were the case? If you slept in that direction it could help you make money, but also make it hard to save at the same time. These contradictions happen to just about everybody.

Finally, even though there are countless feng shui solutions, they all fall into just three major categories.

The first category is to simply *avoid environments that have no remedy.*

There isn't a cure for every single problem; some cures are prohibitively expensive, such as tearing down a building and starting over when it is too dilapidated and awkward to remodel. I once called Master Sang for his input on an office space my clients wanted to lease in one of the triangular-shaped Century City Towers. The suite wrapped around two of the three sides of the triangle and was shaped like a boomerang. Knowing that this was simply a bad shape for an office, I was hoping he could magically pull something out of his arsenal of wisdom to help me make this floor plan situation work. His response: "Tell them to keep looking, find another space."

The second category is to *change the energy of the space.*

This can be accomplished by using Five-Element Theory, such as adding a literal element to a room or changing the colors. This can also be accomplished through applications of yin-yang theory, such as adding a skylight to a perpetually dark area. You can also change the energy of an indoor or outdoor space following the principles of ch'i flow with interior design, furniture placement, and landscaping.

The third category is to *change your personal relationship with the space.*

This book highlighted many ways to position yourself for both sleep and work in order to be as productive as possible, no matter what kind of space you occupy. When you can apply remedies from both the second and third categories, you can often get such a good result that you may not even feel a need to move from the space. In fact, I would not be a feng shui consultant if every situation necessitated a remodel or a move. It would be stressful and depressing to deliver bad news with no practical, immediate, or affordable options. Some remedies cost less than a fancy meal at an expensive restaurant—and it doesn't cost anything to sleep in a different direction!

This is the gift of feng shui: the matrix of working with nature, timing, the elements, and your own infinite creative spirit. You have an aura and soul connection to this planet and the cosmos. It is your birthright. It is another way to inherit the Earth.

ABOUT THE AUTHOR

Kartar Diamond grew up in Southern California in the 1970s and always
had a fascination with metaphysical top-
ics. She has also had an enduring interest
in holistic lifestyle choices and studying
how people are affected by their environment.

In 1992, a chance meeting with
Grand Master Sang began Kartar's formal feng shui studies. She has since
become one of his best-known certified
graduates and instructors. Sang's school,
the American Feng Shui Institute, enjoys
a worldwide reputation as one of the most comprehensive classical feng
shui learning centers.

In 1993, Kartar launched her own consulting business, Feng Shui
Solutions, and routinely works with several hundred clients per year.
Kartar advises on both existing residential and commercial properties
in addition to house-hunting and design phase projects.

Kartar teaches introductory classes at numerous state colleges and
adult schools and came out with her own Traditional Video Workshop
Series in 1999.

Her professional alliances have included the American Society of
Interior Designers and she is referred to by many real estate companies
including Coldwell Banker.

Kartar's lengthy list of speaking engagements has included Barnes & Noble Booksellers, Universal Studios, Xerox Corporation, the Los Angeles Country Club, and USC's Festival of Health, to name a few.

Kartar's books are a manifestation of having studied every branch and style of feng shui, voluminous hands-on experience and case study feedback, as well as a passion for educating the Western world about the benefits of this greatly unknown and misunderstood ancient practice.

Her books stand out for their uniqueness in being able to deliver advanced information in a user-friendly format, prioritize the most important things for readers and consumers to be aware of, as well as for dispelling the myths and superstitions that cloud the integrity of feng shui as a legitimate earth science and healing art.

Kartar's future will undoubtedly include the publishing of more educational materials and delivering this time-honored wisdom to the people who need it most.

Give the Gift of

The Feng Shui Matrix

Another Way to Inherit the Earth

CHECK YOUR LEADING BOOKSTORE OR ORDER HERE

❑ **YES**, I want _____ copies of *The Feng Shui Matrix* at $19.95 each, plus $4.95 shipping per book (CA residents please add $1.64 sales tax per book). Canadian orders must be accompanied by a postal money order in U.S. funds. Allow 15 days for delivery.

My check or money order for $_____ is enclosed.

Please charge my: ❑ Visa ❑ MasterCard

You can also order through PayPal from the **www.FengShuiSolutions.net** website.

Name _____

Organization _____

Address _____

City/State/Zip _____

Phone_____ Email _____

Card # _____

Exp. Date_____ Signature _____

Please make your check payable and return to:
Four Pillars Publishing
3824 Perham Drive • Culver City, CA 90232

Call your credit card order to: 310-842-8870
Fax: 310-842-8914